THE
HOLY
LAND
Devotional

THE
HOLY
LAND
Devotional

Inspirational Reflections
from the Land Where Jesus Walked

JOHN A. BECK

BakerBooks

a division of Baker Publishing Group
Grand Rapids, Michigan

© 2022 by John A. Beck

Published by Baker Books
a division of Baker Publishing Group
PO Box 6287, Grand Rapids, MI 49516-6287
www.bakerbooks.com

Printed in the United States of America

Library of Congress Cataloging-in-Publication Data
Names: Beck, John A., 1956– author.
Title: The Holy Land devotional : inspirational reflections from the land where Jesus walked / John A. Beck.
Other titles: Inspirational reflections from the land where Jesus walked
Description: Grand Rapids, MI : Baker Books, a division of Baker Publishing Group, [2022]
Identifiers: LCCN 2021058121 | ISBN 9781540901811 (paperback) | ISBN 9781493437764 (ebook)
Subjects: LCSH: Christian pilgrims and pilgrimages—Israel—Guidebooks. | Christian pilgrims and pilgrimages—Prayers and devotions. | Bible—Geography. | Israel—Guidebooks.
Classification: LCC DS103 .B35 2022 | DDC 263/.0425694–dc23/eng/20220314
LC record available at https://lccn.loc.gov/2021058121

Scripture quotations are from THE HOLY BIBLE, NEW INTERNATIONAL VERSION®, NIV® Copyright © 1973, 1978, 1984, 2011 by Biblica, Inc.® Used by permission. All rights reserved worldwide.

Baker Publishing Group publications use paper produced from sustainable forestry practices and post-consumer waste whenever possible.

Interior design by William Overbeeke.

22   23   24   25   26   27   28   7   6   5   4   3   2   1

To my loving soul mate, Marmy,
and to all my students who have walked the Holy Land
seeking literacy in the geospeak of God

CONTENTS

Contents

Contents

Contents

INTRODUCTION

Some of what the Lord has to say to us, he has said using the language of geography. It's there on every page of the Bible. But we don't have to read very far before it becomes clear that the Bible is not from around here—at least not our version of "around here." It speaks of ecosystems, weather systems, and cities that we may know next to nothing about.

Yet it is through such language that the Lord reveals himself. He longs for us to know who he is, how he thinks about us, and how he wants us to think about others. In sharing those insights, the biblical authors and poets carefully weave geography into their communication. This means we will not hear all that the Lord has to say to us until we tune our ears to the geospeak of God.

For more than twenty-five years, biblical geography has been the focus of my work. I've studied the role that place plays in Bible communication and shared those insights with my students, readers, and viewers. What I haven't done, until now, is write a devotional guide to the Holy Land.

Unlike my earlier work, *The Holy Land for Christian Travelers*, this book is not a travel guide. Rather, it's a worship tool that can be used by Christian travelers to the Holy Land. I expect your trip will be filled with fun and adventure, a little shopping, and plenty of learning. But I pray it will also include quiet time with the Lord. This book is meant to foster those moments of personal Bible reading and worship, and whether you're sitting at home or walking through your spiritual homeland, it offers dozens of devotions that invite you to hear God speaking in and through the places you visit.

Promised Land

The LORD had said to Abram, "Go from your country, your people and your father's household to the land I will show you."

Genesis 12:1

First words are consequential, so I'm careful as I choose the first words my students hear after landing in Israel. On our bus ride from the airport, I begin by reading Genesis 12:1, the first words we hear the Lord speak to Abraham and Sarah: "Go from your country, your people and your father's household to the land I will show you." Let's consider how these words apply to you as you begin your time in the Holy Land.

Now, it goes without saying that the trip Abraham and Sarah made to the promised land was quite different from anyone's trip to Israel today. Abraham and Sarah didn't fly; they walked nearly four hundred miles. They didn't have an airline ticket with a destination but trekked for weeks without knowing for sure where their journey would end (Heb. 11:8). They didn't selectively pack a suitcase to stay within the airline's prescribed weight limit but gathered up nearly all they owned, driving their sheep, goats, and camels ahead of them. They didn't reach their destination within twenty-four hours but rambled unfamiliar roadways for nearly a month. That is not how your trip to Israel will look!

But there are two similarities between your trip and theirs that I wouldn't want you to miss.

First, your trip to Israel is neither accidental nor the sole product of all the practical decisions you've made leading up to it. Like he did with Abraham and Sarah, the Lord has called you to leave your country and family to visit this land. Whether this means you've purchased an airline ticket, packed a suitcase, and changed time zones or simply walked to your favorite reading chair in the living room, it's no coincidence that you're starting this trip. This is the Lord's doing, and you won't appreciate all that is to come unless you start with that thought in mind.

The second similarity between your trip and that of Abraham and Sarah is the Lord's reason for bringing you to this land. This is a land that the Lord is eager to show you. Throughout the Bible, the Spirit has intimately linked lesson with landscape. And now, in and through the geographic realities of this land, the Lord is poised to speak to you about who he is and how he thinks about you.

Be ready! New insights await you at every turn.

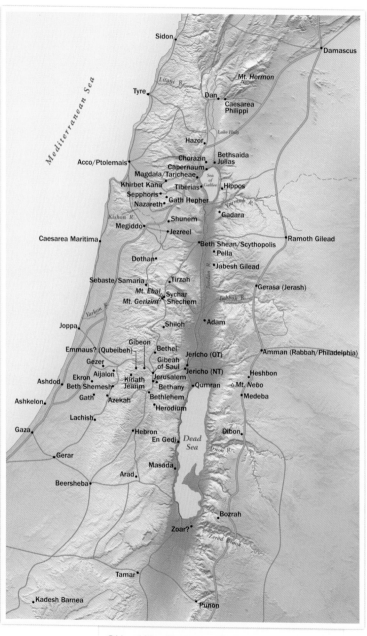

Old and New Testament cities of the promised land.

❧ Where have you already noticed a connection in the Bible between what God says and where he says it?

❧ What place are you most excited to visit in Israel and why?

I'm ready, Lord. I'm excited to begin this trip of a lifetime, a trip you are calling me to take. Please protect me as I travel, and fill me with new insights in this place you desire to show me.

Ashkelon

Ashkelon National Park

JOHN 3:16

For God so loved the world that he gave his one and only Son, that whoever believes in him shall not perish but have eternal life.

John 3:16

Ashkelon! Really? Perhaps you expected me to start the itinerary for our trip with a place you know, like Bethlehem or Jerusalem. I get your reservations. The coastal city of Ashkelon is mentioned only twelve times in the Bible. We meet no one from there by name. We hear no personal stories. In fact, every reference to this Philistine city highlights its hostility toward God's chosen people.

Why start here, then? Well, it comes first alphabetically. But more importantly, Ashkelon and the coastal plain highlight the important role of place in God's plan of salvation.

This bull calf and shrine (sixteenth century BC) that were discovered near the entrance to Ashkelon highlight the city's pagan heritage.

So, what do we know about Ashkelon? First, it was huge. The Canaanite city, which dates to the time of Jacob, was more than twenty times larger than the average Israelite town in the country's mountainous interior.

Second, Ashkelon was wealthy. This coastal harbor was perfectly positioned for business at the meeting point between overland trade routes and the maritime routes connecting to markets around the Mediterranean Sea. It thrived.

You can even hear that in its name: A-*shekel*-on. (The shekel was the unit of weight used by ancient merchants.)

Third, Ashkelon was powerful. The wealth of the city required protection. Because Ashkelon lacked natural defenses on most sides, its earliest citizens built a rampart that surrounded the city—fifty feet tall and nearly one hundred feet wide at the base. It's the first thing visitors saw, and it impresses to this day.

Finally, Ashkelon was pagan. The bull calf shrine built into the defensive wall near the city's entrance highlights its spiritual heritage.

Why did the Lord allow this kind of place to exist in the promised land? You will see the answer if you think spatially. Most Bible stories take place in Israel's mountain interior. Very few stories occur on the coastal plain where the world traveled and traded. While the story of salvation was maturing in the mountains, the Lord kept the world close, right at Israel's doorstep. And when the time was right, even Ashkelon came to know Jesus, for among its ruins we find the foundation stones of early church buildings.

So who is the Lord keeping close to you? The fact of the matter is that the Lord has put people near us—in our neighborhood, at school, or at work—who may seem to have it all. Like Ashkelon, some may even show hostility toward our faith. But they are part of the world Jesus came to forgive. And like Ashkelon, they're the world the Lord has put at our doorstep.

🌾 Where do you see an Ashkelon-like presence the Lord has placed near you?

🌾 How does the city of Ashkelon challenge you to think differently about those living near you who appear to have little need for the gospel?

Lord, help me see that where I live is no accident. You have put me at the doorstep of a world that needs to know you as its Savior. Give me the patience and wisdom to speak to those around me, knowing they are the world you came to save.

Azekah

Tel Azekah

--------- **1 SAMUEL 17:1–16, 32–53** ---------

> The LORD who rescued me from the paw of the lion and the
> paw of the bear will rescue me from the hand of this Philistine.
>
> 1 Samuel 17:37

It's a hike from the parking lot to the top of Tel Azekah. But it's worth all the effort for a commanding view of the battlefield on which David fought Goliath—a story that teaches a lesson on leadership.

Alarm bells were sounding throughout Israel. We can hear them if we know how to listen with our eyes in the opening verses of this story. Perched here on the summit of Azekah, we can see how it all played out. To the west is the coastal plain, homeland of the Philistines. Along the eastern horizon are the central mountains that Israel called home. Between the two lies the Elah Valley, stretching from Azekah through Ephes Dammim to Sokoh (1 Sam. 17:1–3). Water flowing west from the mountains to the Mediterranean Sea cut this

The view east from Azekah captures the setting for David's fight with Goliath, a story that teaches us a lesson on leadership.

serpentine valley through the foothills, creating an invasion path that led directly into the mountain interior Israel called home.

The storyteller uses geography to paint a picture of the unfolding national emergency. The Philistine invaders have left the coast and captured nearly the entire length of the Elah Valley. Saul and the Israelite army are confined to the valley's far eastern side, literally pinned with their backs to the mountain wall. If they were to surrender any more ground, the Philistine invaders would have the run of the mountain interior. Then no Israelite and no place in Israel would be safe.

This kind of national emergency calls for a strong leader. So all eyes in Israel turn to the current king, Saul. But for weeks he has failed to show leadership or inspire the courage needed to drive the enemy from this critical real estate.

Then David arrives, bringing with him all the leadership qualities Saul lacks. David's willingness to fight Goliath shows courage. His choice of weapon demonstrates wisdom. And his words reveal his faith.

Is this kind of leader born or made?

David recognizes how the Lord has been carefully shaping him for this moment: "The LORD who rescued me from the paw of the lion and the paw of the bear will rescue me from the hand of this Philistine" (1 Sam. 17:37). Every time a bear or lion had threatened the family's livestock, the Lord had used it to advance the character and courage of this young man who would one day be Israel's second king.

The Lord may be doing a similar thing for us today. As you and I confront unwanted challenges, he is instilling courage, growing wisdom, and maturing faith for a time when we, too, may be called on to lead in a crucial moment.

🐾 What life experiences has the Lord been using to shape your character for service in his kingdom?

🐾 What leadership qualities has the Lord developed in you?

🐾 Where do you see the opportunity to lead?

Honestly, Lord, most days I don't feel much
like a leader. Others seem better suited to that role
than I do. Help me see more clearly the ways you
have shaped my character for leadership, and point
me to those places where you have prepared me to
lead.

Beersheba

Tel Beersheba National Park

GENESIS 46:1–7

Do not be afraid to go down to Egypt, for I will make you into a great nation there. I will go down to Egypt with you, and I will surely bring you back again. And Joseph's own hand will close your eyes.

Genesis 46:3–4

E very time I stand at Beersheba looking south into the dry reaches of the Negev basin, I feel the tension that must have welled up in Jacob. Here he faced one of the most consequential decisions of his life.

On the one hand, Jacob knew he should stay put. The Lord made a promise to Jacob's grandparents, Abraham and Sarah, who had been childless at the time. He promised that their family would grow into a great nation and that he would give them the land of Canaan as their homeland. From this nation on this land, the Lord promised to restore the blessing that had been lost in Eden (Gen. 12:1–7). It's unthinkable that Jacob would leave. The altar his father, Isaac, had built here at Beersheba reminded him of God's promised plan of

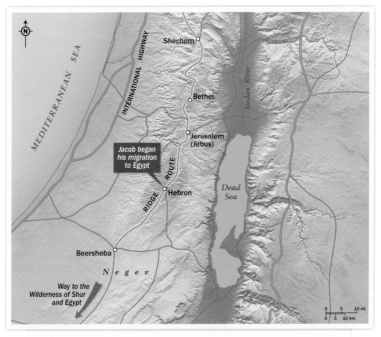

Jacob faced a decision at Beersheba that would have far-reaching consequences.

salvation (26:23–25). But there is something else—something that isn't apparent from our modern view. Beersheba was the southernmost city of the promised land (Judg. 20:1; 1 Sam. 3:20). One more step south and Jacob would be leaving the land he was never supposed to leave.

On the other hand, Jacob knew he had to go. A seven-year famine had gripped the land of Canaan. In a bid to ward off starvation, Jacob had twice sent his sons to purchase grain from Egypt, but this was a stopgap measure at best. They needed to migrate to survive.

The matter was further complicated by the story of Jacob's son Joseph. Jacob thought Joseph was dead. But when his sons returned from Egypt after a second trip to purchase grain, Jacob learned that Joseph was alive and had risen to political prominence. Now Joseph was beckoning his family to travel to Egypt, where he would personally care for them.

With famine driving him from the land and the promise of reunion pulling him from the land, Jacob knew he had to go.

Just imagine the tension Jacob experienced at Beersheba. Only then will we appreciate the moment the Lord breaks the unbearable stress with these words: "Do not be afraid to go down to Egypt, for I will make you into a great nation there" (Gen. 46:3). Jacob was free to depart Canaan. There would be an Egyptian extension to the plan of salvation.

While God always has a plan, we might not always be able to see it. And that generates a great deal of inner turmoil when we face a consequential decision at our own "Beersheba." When we stand at such a border place, shifting our weight from one foot to the other, we can do what Jacob did: stop, worship, and listen for the answer. The Lord will meet us at the border and signal the turn he wants us to take.

🌿 When have you felt tension over a choice like the one Jacob faced at Beersheba?

🌿 What did you do well and what did you do poorly in making your decision?

🌿 How did the Lord make the path forward clear to you?

Lord, I don't like feeling the tension of being caught between two choices at the border. I want to rush ahead and just get the decision made so that life can move forward. Please give me the patience I lack to hold that decision in tension until you make the path forward clear.

Beth Shean/ Scythopolis

Beth Shean National Park

LUKE 12:13–21

Then he said to them, "Watch out! Be on your guard against all kinds of greed; life does not consist in an abundance of possessions."

Luke 12:15

Six thousand years! That's how long there has been a major city at this intersection of the Jordan and Jezreel Valleys. Established hundreds of years before Abraham's birth, the city was first called Beth Shean. Its successor, Scythopolis, was still going strong at the time of Jesus. So far as we know, Jesus never visited this prosperous Decapolis city. But he does warn us against adopting its worldly values.

Beth Shean/Scythopolis was destined to become something special. Its location at the junction of two major valley systems meant that merchants carrying commodities between Saudi Arabia, Egypt, Europe, and Asia had to travel through it. The city's spectacular wealth and the culture of greed that it fostered are intimately tied to its advantageous geography.

Scythopolis wasn't shy about showing off its wealth. Instead of the meandering dirt streets that were typical in Galilean villages at the time of Jesus, Scythopolis had boulevards paved with basalt blocks laid in a herringbone pattern. Unlike in the subsistence economy of surrounding towns, where people worked endlessly to meet their basic needs, residents of Scythopolis simply purchased whatever they needed. Shoppers strolled on pillar-lined sidewalks decorated with inlaid mosaics as they shopped for food, clothing, and luxury items.

Palladius Street in Scythopolis, a city that possessed everything except eternal satisfaction.

Instead of having to dig and maintain wells, citizens of Scythopolis could walk to the city center, where piped-in water gushed from an ornate fountain. When nature called, they didn't have to discreetly walk out of the village but could saunter down the block to an enclosed public restroom complete with ancient toilet seats. Typical villages didn't offer much in the way of entertainment, but Scythopolis boasted a bathhouse, a theater, and a chariot racetrack. Oh yes, Scythopolis seemed to have it all.

But having it all didn't bring satisfaction, as one disembodied voice from the past makes clear. A man who lived in another Decapolis city that was similar to Scythopolis carved these words on the lintel of his grave: "After all things, a tomb." There was a void in his life that could not be filled by material luxuries.

Jesus said it like this: "Life does not consist in an abundance of possessions" (Luke 12:15). And that's still true for each of us today. I have stood at Scythopolis beside people whose eyes filled with tears as they told me about their former life of having everything that money could buy. But until they found Jesus, they lacked the true satisfaction found not in an abundance of possessions but in having the one thing we need most: Jesus.

🐾 Why do we so easily fall into the trap of thinking that more possessions will bring us more happiness?

🐾 What do you do to keep your views on material possessions aligned with those expressed by Jesus?

Lord Jesus, I am so easily entrapped by the love of things. I confess that abundant possessions will not lead to satisfaction in life or hope for the life to come. Please save me from myself. Anchor my identity and satisfaction in you.

Beth Shemesh

Tel Beth Shemesh

──── **1 SAMUEL 6:7–20** ────

And the people of Beth Shemesh asked, "Who can stand in the presence of the LORD, this holy God? To whom will the ark go up from here?"

1 Samuel 6:20

T he Bible is the only ancient book to mention Beth Shemesh. And this narrative in 1 Samuel 6 mentions it more frequently than any other Bible story: nine times in twelve verses. We know we must be on to something special, but in this case the something special is not something good.

Since the opening verses of 1 Samuel 4, the narrator has focused our attention on an object rather than a person: the ark of the covenant. Previous Old Testament books tell us that this piece of Israelite worship furniture should be tucked safely inside the Most Holy Place of the sanctuary at Shiloh. Instead, we see Israel taking the ark into battle like a talisman

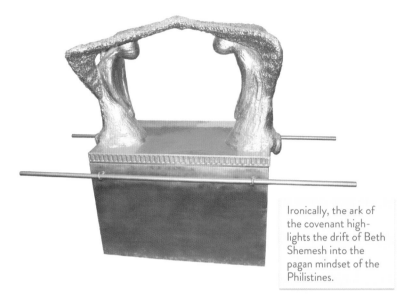

Ironically, the ark of the covenant high-lights the drift of Beth Shemesh into the pagan mindset of the Philistines.

and then fumbling it into the hands of the Philistines, where for seven months it was passed around among their pagan cities. These troubling scenes come as a direct consequence of Israel's drift into the pagan mindset of their neighbors.

In 1 Samuel 6, we read how the Philistines finally return the ark to Israel. "Now the people of Beth Shemesh were harvesting their wheat in the valley, and when they looked up and saw the ark, they rejoiced at the sight" (v. 13). There is reason to celebrate, particularly because the ark is approaching Beth Shemesh. And here's the reason for the town's repeated mention in the story: Beth Shemesh is no ordinary town. Beth Shemesh is one of the Levitical towns (Josh. 21:16). Who better to know how to handle the ark than Israel's religious educators?

But the celebration is short-lived, because the Levites decide to crack open the box and look inside. Only the high priest was allowed to see the ark of the covenant, and then only once a year, on the Day of Atonement (Lev. 16). This egregious violation at Beth Shemesh causes the Lord to strike out in anger, and seventy people die.

Here is what I find so arresting. The Levites, who should have been fully trained in handling the ark, did little better with it than the pagan Philistines. And when they became frustrated with it, they did exactly what the Philistines did: they moved the ark on to the next city. Ironically, that next city where the ark would remain for twenty years, Kiriath Jearim, was *not* a Levitical city (1 Sam. 6:21–7:1).

Beth Shemesh was poised to be the hero of this story, but it quickly becomes a symbol of all that is wrong with the story evolving in Israel. And that makes this a cautionary tale that still speaks to us. The people of Beth Shemesh treated sacred things as poorly as their pagan neighbors. Have we done something as egregious?

🌿 As a believer, what sacred things and thoughts have been put into your care?

🌿 God expects us to live and think differently than our pagan neighbors and coworkers. Where have you seen those expected differences breaking down?

Heavenly Father, I have the privilege of knowing you for who you are. I pray that while I live in the world, I maintain my separation from the world. Help your church and its leaders to honor and care for the sacred things you have brought into our lives.

Bethany
Church of Saint Lazarus

"Martha, Martha," the Lord answered, "you are worried and upset about many things, but few things are needed—or indeed only one. Mary has chosen what is better, and it will not be taken away from her."

Luke 10:41–42

When I approach the Church of Saint Lazarus in Bethany, my eyes meet the gazes of three figures looking down from the mosaic façade of the modern church. We know them as Mary, Martha, and Lazarus, a family from Bethany whom Jesus visited on at least two occasions. The two Bethany stories told in Luke 10 and John 11 join hands to teach a powerful lesson about listening to Jesus.

In Luke 10, when Jesus and his entourage arrive in Bethany, it triggers a series of social obligations. Martha responds by opening her home to them (v. 38). As the household's senior female member, she understands all that such an invitation involves: she has to acquire enough food, prepare the meals, and serve all her guests. It's a big job, and she is counting on the help of her sister, Mary.

When Jesus enters the house and begins to teach, the two sisters choose different paths. Mary quickly abandons her other duties to sit at Jesus's feet and listen. Martha's response is different: surely she can work and listen at the same time. After all, the house is small—a mere four hundred square feet. Certain she has made the better choice, the frustrated Martha urges Jesus to help her get Mary back to work. Instead, she gets an unexpected scolding. Jesus criticizes Martha's distracted multitasking and boldly states that Mary has made the better choice. Ouch!

Nothing more is said on the matter until we return to Bethany in John 11. Lazarus, the brother of Mary and Martha, has died. As grief grips both sisters, the consequences of Martha's distracted listening surface. Martha hears that Jesus is approaching the village and sets out to meet him. She has something to say: "If you had been here, my brother would not have died" (v. 21).

Jesus counters with hope: "Your brother will rise again" (v. 23). Perhaps recalling Jesus's earlier criticism, Martha insists that she had been listening. She repeatedly says that she *knows* this.

But Jesus asks her, "Do you believe this?" (v. 26), and again, "Did I not tell you that if you believe, you will see the glory of God?" (v. 40).

When we bring these two Bethany stories together, it becomes clear that Martha's distracted listening had left her knowing but struggling to believe.

I tend to be more like Martha than Mary. Perhaps you do as well. I always have more to do than time in which to

The Church of Saint Lazarus in Bethany invites us to link two stories from the lives of Mary, Martha, and Lazarus.

do it. So I attempt to multitask, even though it leads to the kind of distraction that harms the quality of everything I'm doing. Sadly, this can even affect my reading of God's Word. Have you fallen into the same trap?

🎵 How have you noticed your listening to Jesus being impaired by distraction?

🎵 Where have you experienced the difference between knowing and believing when managing a challenge in life?

Lord Jesus, I feel the heavy press of responsibility. Like Martha, I want to both get things done and listen to you. Help me to shift my priorities so that I can listen in the undistracted way of Mary. Help me to know and to believe.

Bethany

Tomb of Lazarus

I am the resurrection and the life. The one who believes in me will live, even though they die; and whoever lives by believing in me will never die.

John 11:25–26

Bethany never lets us stray far from its signature story. The name of the modern town, El-Azariyeh, pays homage to Lazarus. The traditional tomb of Lazarus awaits visitors. And the modern Church of Saint Lazarus in Bethany resembles an echoey tomb adorned with art that tells the story of the raising of Lazarus. Bethany wasn't the first or only place where Jesus raised the dead, but it may be the best place to reflect on loss and hope.

The story in John 11 is an authentic depiction of loss. The early mention of Lazarus's illness (v. 3) quickly gives way to the unexpected news of his death (v. 14). We can picture the surreal walk from the family's home to the cemetery

The traditional tomb of Lazarus in Bethany invites us to think about loss and hope.

for Lazarus's burial, which in first-century Jewish culture took place the same day he died (v. 31). We smell the odor of decomposition (v. 39). We see raw emotion on display even in Jesus, whose body shuddered with grief as he wept at the tomb (v. 35). We see denial and despair. Jewish tradition held that a person's life force remained near the deceased's body through the third day. During those days, the family hoped for a miracle. But by day four, denial gave way to despair (vv. 17, 39). And woven throughout is the human tendency of blaming someone, anyone, for the vexing loss, given that matters of life and death lie beyond mortal control (vv. 21, 32, 37). If there's a place that can show us what loss looks like, Bethany is that place.

But Bethany is also the place to find hope. Jesus delays coming to Bethany until after Lazarus has died, but when he arrives he makes this powerful declaration: "I am the resurrection and the life. The one who believes in me will live, even though they die; and whoever lives by believing in me will never die" (John 11:25–26).

And when Jesus arrives at the tomb with Mary and Martha, our Savior puts those words into action and summons Lazarus to come out. No worse for wear, Lazarus does as he's told.

This powerful Bethany story leaves no doubt that the horrible wedge death drives between us and those we love is not permanent. To be sure, death brings pain, grief, and uncertainty, just as it did to Lazarus's loved ones. But we do not grieve without hope. Bethany reminds us that reunion is coming.

🐾 Where do you see your grief experience illustrated in this Bethany story?

🐾 How can you use this story to help others who are struggling with the loss of a loved one?

Jesus, you know what it is to love and what it feels like to lose a loved one. But only you can replace death with life, separation with reunion. Comfort and encourage me today.

Bethlehem

Church of the Nativity

LUKE 2:1–20

> So Joseph also went up from the town of Nazareth in Galilee to
> Judea, to Bethlehem the town of David, because he belonged
> to the house and line of David.
>
> Luke 2:4

Could there be a Christmas story without Bethlehem? Not if Luke has anything to say about it.
Luke tells the Christmas story with extreme
economy in Luke 2:1–20. He leaves out many more details
than he mentions, but there's one detail he insists we get right.
Five times in just twenty verses, Luke mentions the place
Jesus was born—a place marked today by the Church of the
Nativity in Bethlehem. He refers to Bethlehem as Joseph's
"own town" (v. 3) and "the town of David" (v. 4). The angels
direct the shepherds to "the town of David" (v. 11), and the
shepherds report they are headed for "Bethlehem" (v. 15).

Clearly, Bethlehem is vital to the story.

The star beneath this altar in the Church of the Nativity marks the traditional birthplace of Jesus in Bethlehem, a town vital to the Christmas story.

To appreciate its importance, we need to think about it through the lens of the Old Testament. Let's start with the book of Ruth, which is a story that largely unfolds in Bethlehem and formally mentions the name of this town seven times. Here in this Judean town, two women faced social and economic obstacles that threatened their survival. But here the Lord solved their problems through the kindly care of Boaz.

Two generations later, the spotlight was back on Bethlehem, only instead of a family in need, we see a nation in need. Saul, Israel's first king, failed to keep his focus on Israel's national mission and imperiled his people by allowing the Philistines to persistently invade their homeland. So the Lord sent the prophet Samuel to address the problem. He traveled to Bethlehem and anointed David as Saul's replacement. The town is formally mentioned three times in this story (1 Sam. 16:1, 4, 18).

A little more than 250 years later, Israel's leaders were failing again. The prophet Micah took them to task but also pointed to the coming of better days when a new leader would emerge. He spoke directly of a coming Messiah who would be born in Bethlehem (Mic. 5:2).

For Old Testament readers, one thing is clear: Bethlehem persists as a place where the Lord provides solutions for people in crisis, whether that be a family, a nation, or the world.

And that's why Luke mentions Bethlehem so often. On that first Christmas Eve, when Mary laid her newborn son in a manger in Bethlehem, we know that we have witnessed something special. Bethlehem isn't just the place where Jesus was born; it's a place that shapes our impression of his birth. Luke's story shows Bethlehem bringing the best solution of all: salvation from sin.

🐑 Places have personalities. How would you describe the personality of Bethlehem?

🐑 How does the personality of Bethlehem contribute to your understanding of the Christmas story?

Lord, I thought I had the details of the Christmas story down—the manger, Mary, Joseph, the shepherds, the angels, and the baby Jesus. But now I see that Bethlehem is part of this story as well. Please give me and my family the solution for sin that you offer there.

Bethlehem

Manger Square

> May the LORD make the woman who is coming into your home like Rachel and Leah, who together built up the family of Israel. May you have standing in Ephrathah and be famous in Bethlehem.
>
> Ruth 4:11

Manger Square in Bethlehem is a meaningful place to think about the Christmas story. But as we rub shoulders with pilgrims from all over the world, this square is also a place to think about immigrants and foreigners.

Depending on which Old Testament texts we read, we're left with differing impressions of non-Israelites. On the one hand, foreigners and immigrants are extended legal protection within Israel (Exod. 22:21; Lev. 19:33–34). On the other hand, the prophets rain down chapter-long judgment speeches on people from places like Moab (Isa. 15:1–16:14;

49

Jer. 48:1–47). That tension is broken in the story of Ruth the Moabite, who made her home in Bethlehem.

A cascade of tragedies sets the stage for the book of Ruth. Naomi and her husband, Elimelech, had enjoyed the good life offered in Bethlehem, a place known for its agricultural bounty. But instead of celebrating the grain harvest, the opening verses of the book of Ruth highlight the awful famine gripping the land of Israel. Naomi and her family abandon their homestead in Bethlehem and trudge east across the Jordan River valley and onto the high plateau of Moab, where they find food and also brides for their two sons. Life is passably better for a time.

A threshing floor near Bethlehem sets the stage for Ruth's marriage to Boaz and offers a glimpse into the Lord's perspective on immigrants.

Then tragedy strikes again when Naomi's husband and two sons die. Grief-stricken and discouraged by multiple losses, Naomi decides to return to Bethlehem, and her daughter-in-law Ruth goes with her. Grain again grows in the fields around Bethlehem, but access is another issue, because during Naomi's absence others laid claim to her family's farmland. So, despite the risk involved (Ruth 2:9, 22), Ruth the Moabite goes out to glean in the Bethlehem fields, hoping to find a meager amount of grain to support her and Naomi (2:2).

Ruth's gleaning sets the stage for the Lord to clarify his perspective on non-Israelites who have immigrated into the promised land. The vulnerable Ruth is never accosted because the Lord keeps her safe under the watchful eyes of Boaz. The kindness of this Bethlehem local is contagious, and soon other people in town begin to treat Ruth like one of their own. They even go so far as to speak a blessing over her that likens her to their own forebearers, Rachel and Leah (Ruth 4:11).

And soon after Ruth and Boaz marry, this immigrant woman becomes intimately bound to the story of salvation. Ruth the Moabite is the great-grandmother of King David and a forebearer of Jesus.

It's easy to become suspicious of those who are unlike us, particularly those who come from other places. But in the actions and attitude of Boaz, we are given an example of how the Lord wants us to treat them. May we follow his lead in offering protection, provision, and respect to the immigrant and foreigner.

🐝 How are the lives of immigrants today similar to and different from the life of Ruth?

🐝 In what ways is the Lord calling you to follow in the footsteps of Boaz and care for the immigrant and foreigner among us?

Lord, we confess that differences between ourselves and others have generated fear and mistreatment. Help me to see foreigners as you see them. Help me to treat immigrants as Boaz treated Ruth.

Bethlehem
Shepherds' Fields

> But the angel said to them, "Do not be afraid."
>
> Luke 2:10

When on a trip to the Holy Land, the question is not whether you should visit Bethlehem but where you should start your visit. I prefer starting from the agricultural fields east of town, which is where the Lord made the meaning of Christmas clear.

Many people choose to begin their visit at the Church of the Nativity in the heart of modern Bethlehem, the traditional location of Jesus's birth. To be fair, that's where Luke starts the familiar Christmas story in chapter 2 of his Gospel. But at verse 8, he shifts the scene to the agricultural fields that fill the basin east of the spur on which the town was built. There a collection of shepherds had moved their hungry livestock into the harvested grain fields and were just settling in for the night.

Then it happened. This pastoral setting changed abruptly with the appearance of a single angel. That's all it took. The shepherds were terrified.

Their response takes us back hundreds of pages in the Bible and thousands of years in time to the first mention of fear in the Old Testament. The garden of Eden was intended to be a fear-free zone. Created in God's image, Adam and Eve thought as God thought and saw the world as God saw it. Sin was the only thing missing from the garden in which they lived. And because there was an absence of sin, there was also an absence of fear.

But that all changed when Adam and Eve took fruit from the forbidden tree. Now creation and Creator were no longer in sync. Sin had arrived, and that sin birthed fear. As the Lord approached, Adam and Eve hid themselves, and Adam gave voice to a new reality: "I was afraid" (Gen. 3:10).

That legacy of fear from the garden of Eden lived in the hearts of everyone from Adam to the Christmas shepherds. Every time the Lord or one of his emissaries appeared, sinful people thought the Lord had come to punish their sin.

Christmas changed that, which is why I like to start my Bethlehem visit in the Shepherds' Fields. While the first words spoken by fallen sinners were "I was afraid," the first message God sent to earth following the birth of Jesus was "You can stop being afraid."

To be sure, punishment for sin would come. But that punishment would now be deflected from the sinner to the sinless Savior. Christ's birth meant that all people throughout all time could live free of fear because a Savior was born

The Shepherds' Fields near Bethlehem, where the shepherds heard the angel's message: "Do not be afraid."

in Bethlehem. The terror that filled the shepherds quickly evaporated, even as the one angel was joined by a sky full of the heavenly host. Unlike Adam and Eve, the shepherds did not look for a place to hide but sought direct contact with the God who came to save: "Let's go to Bethlehem and see this thing that has happened" (Luke 2:15).

Jesus's birth means we can fearlessly do the same.

🌺 What sin from your past still makes you afraid to be in the Lord's presence?

🌺 How does the message of the Christmas angel speak to that fear?

Like Adam and the Christmas shepherds, I am afraid, Lord. I feel horrified by the thought of standing before you as one who has regularly and egregiously sinned. Please fill me with a passion to be at your side in Bethlehem because you have come to take away my fear.

Bethphage
Church of Bethphage

LUKE 19:28–34

Go to the village ahead of you, and as you enter it, you will find a colt tied there, which no one has ever ridden. Untie it and bring it here. If anyone asks you, "Why are you untying it?" say, "The Lord needs it."

Luke 19:30–31

The atmosphere was charged long before Jesus got to Bethphage. It was Passover, a festival that brought thousands of excited worshipers to Jerusalem. But on that first Palm Sunday, the excitement escalated to new levels when Jesus rode a donkey into Bethphage.

This is a story on the move, so let's make sure we set it against its changing landscape. Jesus had spent the night in Bethany. He rose early and climbed the east side of the Mount of Olives en route to Jerusalem, which lay on the opposite side of this two-mile-long ridge. Near the ridge's crest was the village of Bethphage.

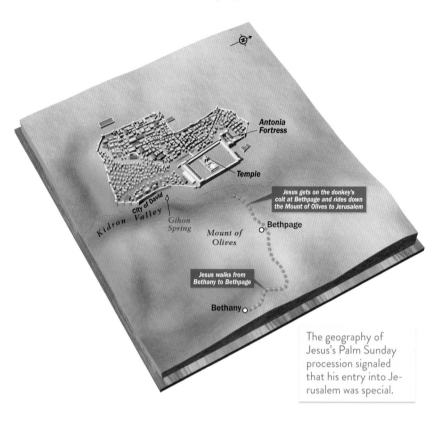

The geography of Jesus's Palm Sunday procession signaled that his entry into Jerusalem was special.

Prior to arriving at Bethphage, Jesus sent two of his disciples ahead to secure a donkey he could ride into the village. This looks strange at several levels. First, it's the only time we read of Jesus riding on an animal. Second, he had just hiked up a steeply pitched slope for twenty minutes, and only now does he want a donkey to ride on. Third, he verbally insists that he "needs it" (Luke 19:31, 34).

The book of Zechariah holds the key to decoding the mystery. Some 550 years before Jesus's birth, this prophet spoke to Israelites who had just returned from exile in Babylon. He prophesied of the future Messiah's arrival in Jerusalem, and the similarities to Palm Sunday are striking. The Messiah would enter the Holy City "lowly and riding on a donkey, on a colt, the foal of a donkey" (Zech. 9:9).

The role of the donkey in the Palm Sunday story is easier to understand than the role of Bethphage, so let's dig deeper into the geography. Zechariah prophesied not only that the Messiah would ride a donkey but also that he would ride it across the city limits and into Jerusalem. So where were the city limits of Jerusalem in the first century? Its defensive walls might seem like a good guess, but the Palm Sunday celebration was already underway on the Mount of Olives, long before Jesus got anywhere near the city walls.

Early Jewish writings describe a different location for Jerusalem's city limits: Bethphage at the crest of the Mount of Olives. That's why Jesus sends the disciples ahead and has them bring a donkey to him *before* he arrives at Bethphage. And that's why the ecstatic welcome of that first Palm Sunday begins the moment word circulates that Jesus has ridden a donkey *into* Bethphage.

It may be easier to picture the donkey than the place, but the story of Palm Sunday has an important geographical dimension. As is often the case, geography isn't just incidental but integral to the telling of this story.

- What does this story teach you about the importance of geography when reading a familiar Bible story?

- What steps can you take to become more familiar with the geography the Bible writers use to shape their message?

I don't want to miss anything, Lord. And it's clear that if I ignore the geography in the Bible, I'll miss some of what you are saying. Tune my sensitivity to all the ways you speak to me, even the geographical ways, so that I may hear you more clearly.

Caesarea Maritima

Caesarea National Park

ACTS 10:19–35, 44–48; 11:17–18

When they heard this, they had no further objections and praised God, saying, "So then, even to Gentiles God has granted repentance that leads to life."

Acts 11:18

The early church was stuck in a mode of thinking that impeded the reach of the gospel. That needed to change, and it did when Peter met with the household of Cornelius in Caesarea Maritima.

By all accounts, this meeting should never have occurred. Peter was in Joppa, the Old Testament seaport on the Mediterranean coast. As a Jewish fisherman, he must have felt at home here among the city's boats and sailors. The streets and wharfs pulsed with people who shared his habits of thought and worship, including a general disdain for gentiles (Acts 10:28).

By contrast, Cornelius was a gentile, a Roman army officer, who lived up the coast in Caesarea Maritima. Here Herod the Great had built the largest seaport in the eastern Mediterranean, which he used to import the culture and ideology of Europe to the coast of Israel. The city contained temples to multiple deities, including the one that soared above Caesarea's harbor and was dedicated to the worship of the Roman emperor.

Cornelius was different from most gentiles in Caesarea. He had sidestepped the polytheistic Roman culture and attached himself to the one God of the Jewish religion as a gentile God-fearer. And this very fact would have made him suspicious of Peter. To Cornelius, Peter's speaking of Jesus as God may well have sounded like a rejection of monotheism

Caesarea on the Mediterranean Sea, the gentile city that changed the church.

and a return to the pagan pantheon he had left behind. All in all, the chances of Peter and Cornelius having a productive meeting in either Joppa or Caesarea seemed remote.

That is, until the Lord intervened. The Lord sent visions to both Peter and Cornelius that began to break down barriers. When Peter eventually made the thirty-two-mile walk north along the coast to Caesarea, something stunning happened: a second Pentecost. Peter preached, the Holy Spirit was poured out, and people spoke in tongues and were baptized. And what's so striking is that this Jerusalem-like experience happened in a thoroughly gentile place.

Turns out, that was the point. And Peter got it. "I now realize how true it is that God does not show favoritism but accepts from every nation the one who fears him and does what is right" (Acts 10:34–35).

But the news of Peter's foray to Caesarea landed with a thud in Jerusalem. The Jewish-Christian church leaders summoned Peter to the Holy City to explain his actions. When he did, the church also recognized that this Pentecost-like event called for a change in how they thought about the kingdom of God: "So then, even to Gentiles God has granted repentance that leads to life" (Acts 11:18).

The Lord used Caesarea Maritima to bring about change in the early church. And we can use it to correct our perspective if we hold the false notion that some people are excluded from God's kingdom.

🌿 Where do you see ethnic barriers still preventing the advance of the gospel?

❧ What can you do to overcome those barriers so that the gospel reaches all people?

Lord Jesus, I know that you suffered and died for the sins of all people, but I confess that I often act as if you did not. Help me break down the barriers that prevent your gospel from reaching all people in all places.

Caesarea Philippi

Banias Nature Reserve

MATTHEW 16:13–18

Simon Peter answered, "You are the Messiah, the Son of the living God."

Matthew 16:16

The Bible and archaeology join to tell the same unattractive story. The region of Caesarea Philippi at the base of Mount Hermon had a persistent problem. Throughout its history, it was a place where people perpetuated a grave misunderstanding of who God is. And it's that misunderstanding that drew Jesus and the disciples there.

The problem began with the Canaanites, who worshiped Baal on Mount Hermon, calling it "Mount Baal Hermon" (Judg. 3:3). We expect things to improve with Israel's arrival, but they did not. King Jeroboam I, the first king of the newly formed northern kingdom, established a worship center at Dan that did more to confuse than clarify. Jeroboam feared his subjects would reunite with the southern kingdom if they traveled to worship the Lord at the temple in Jerusalem, so he set up alternate worship sites at Dan and Bethel. These worship centers were made to look like the temple in Jerusalem but combined worship of the Lord with the worship of Baal (1 Kings 12:26–30). The calf sanctuary at Dan, like its pagan counterparts, misled worshipers and tarnished this region's reputation for the remainder of the Old Testament era.

In the third century BC, Greco-Roman worshipers contributed to the entrenched theological confusion of this region. The southern toe of Mount Hermon terminates in a multicolored, 131-foot cliff face. Recessed into it is a yawning cave that is 66 feet wide by 49 feet tall. In the first century AD, a thundering stream poured out of this cave. To this day it looks surreal and otherworldly, and that appearance had led the ancients to worship the pagan nature deity Pan here.

Just before Jesus was born, Herod the Great added another layer of confusion regarding God's identity. At the base of Mount Hermon, he built a marble-studded temple to the Roman emperor in support of the mistaken notion that the emperor was divine. Failure again! Every time we visit this region of Caesarea Philippi in the Old Testament era, we encounter places and stories that expose confusion about God's identity.

That's why it's so fitting that Jesus takes the disciples here to ask, "Who do you say I am?" And in this place that had so persistently gotten God wrong, we hear testimony that gets it right. The Spirit-filled Peter declares, "You are the Messiah, the Son of the living God" (Matt. 16:15–16).

This is a thunderbolt from heaven. For the first time, the region entertains a statement that accurately portrays God

This beautiful cliff face was the site of a temple to Pan, which only perpetuated the region's confusion about divine identity.

as he is. Jesus seizes the moment. When he tells Peter, "On this rock I will build my church, and the gates of Hades will not overcome it" (Matt. 16:18), he does not mean on "*this* rock"—that is, the mountain face that had been the site of so many misperceptions about God. Rather, he will build his church on the rock of Peter's confession so that not even death itself ("the gates of Hades") will overcome it.

Foundations are important to buildings and to belief systems. Here at Caesarea Philippi, Jesus declares that nothing is more important to the church and to our faith than a correct understanding of who God is.

🌿 What are some places today that persistently mis-represent God?

🌿 How can we keep a correct understanding of God as the foundation of our beliefs?

There are so many paths that mislead. God, help me see you for who you are. Give me a correct understanding so that I can build securely on the foundation that confesses Jesus as Lord.

Capernaum
Archaeology

MARK 2:1–12

But I want you to know that the Son of Man has authority on earth to forgive sins.

Mark 2:10

The people of Capernaum knew Jesus as a Bible teacher, but this story from Mark 2 shows that he was much more.

If we listen, we can hear the friends of the paralyzed man sighing. They had carried their disabled friend to the family compound where Jesus was staying but saw no easy way to get inside. Houses in the Sea of Galilee basin looked different from those built in other places around the promised land. Such first-century dwellings are called *insulae* houses. They were built to accommodate extended families and were designed with a large open-air courtyard (called an *insula*, Latin for "island") surrounded by smaller roofed rooms, each with a single doorway that opened into the courtyard. We

69

These *insulae* houses in Capernaum are where Jesus performed a miracle that set him apart from other religious authorities.

can trace this floor plan in the tangled ancient foundations at the heart of Capernaum.

In this story, Jesus was in one of the side rooms. A sea of people filled the courtyard and prevented the man's friends from getting him anywhere near the one they knew could help.

The exceptional number of people gathered here had to do with the high-stakes meeting underway in the crowded compound. A delegation of teachers had come from Jerusalem to investigate a rogue Bible teacher named Jesus. Within first-century Judaism, the authority to teach was granted by someone who already had that authorization. The schools in Jerusalem did the credentialing, and Jesus wasn't one of their graduates. He was speaking out of turn, and they had come to stop him.

If this were any other story, we might expect the friends to leave and try again another day. We might expect Jesus to capitulate to the Jerusalem authorities. But this is no ordinary story. Pieces of the roof began falling into the middle of the meeting, then a few beams of light penetrated, then a mat swung back and forth as it was lowered into the room on ropes. Undeterred by the crowded courtyard, the roof, or the importance of the meeting, the four friends had solved the access problem.

That's when Jesus took things to a whole different level and addressed a problem that others did not see: "Son, your sins are forgiven" (Mark 2:5). The religious authorities huffed. No human authority, even those credentialed by Jerusalem, would dare stand in the place of God and offer forgiveness.

Could Jesus forgive sin? Yes, and what he said and did next proves it. "'But I want you to know that the Son of Man has authority on earth to forgive sins.' So he said to the man, 'I tell you, get up, take your mat and go home'" (2:10–11). Then those standing closest to the door gasped as the crowd slowly parted and the man they saw being carried to the roof on a mat walked out with the mat in hand.

We live in a noisy world filled with voices making promises and claiming the authority to back them up. "Use this diet plan and lose weight." "Wear this shoe and be a better athlete." But who has the authority to make a promise they can keep every time? Jesus. His is the voice I want to hear.

🐝 What other popular teachers compete with Jesus for your attention?

🐝 How can you be certain that you regard the teaching of Jesus as unique and authoritative?

Lord, there are so many voices offering me advice and direction. It's easy for me to place them on an equal level with the revelation you offer in your Word and through the words of Jesus. Please use this moment to distinguish your voice from any competitors.

Capernaum
Lakeshore

Leaving Nazareth, he went and lived in Capernaum, which was
by the lake in the area of Zebulun and Naphtali.

Matthew 4:13

Nazareth to Capernaum! Did you feel the shock-
wave? If not, I'd like to use these words from Matthew 4:13 to show you what a powerful role geography plays in the Bible's communication.

There's more to this move than first meets the eye, because
Nazareth and Capernaum are radically different places. Nazareth is a rural, agricultural village nestled into a valley on
top of a high ridge. Capernaum is a suburban commercial
center situated on a sprawling plain on the northwest shore
of the Sea of Galilee. Nazareth is isolated and mostly invis-
ible from the world. Capernaum is exposed to the world and
benefits from connection to it. Nazareth belongs to the tribal
territory of Zebulun and Capernaum to the tribal territory
of Naphtali (Josh. 19:10–16, 32–39).

The fact that Jesus traded Nazareth for a totally different place begs for further comment, and Matthew is happy to oblige. He explains how Jesus's move fulfills an Old Testament prophecy about the Messiah. The hard part? Matthew uses more geography to explain the geography!

Centuries earlier, the promised land had been divided into twelve tribal allotments, which included the territories of Zebulun and Naphtali. In the eighth century BC, both were experiencing dark days. The invasion of the Assyrian Empire had so impacted this region that it became known as "Galilee of the Gentiles."

Jesus's move from Nazareth to Capernaum positioned the gospel so that it would reach each of us.

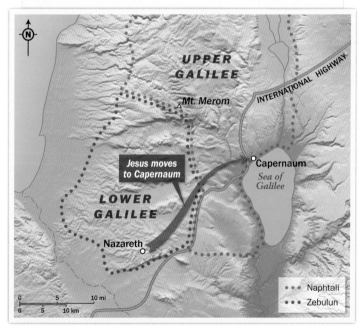

However, Isaiah prophesied of a time when this regional darkness would give way to the light of the Messiah's arrival (Isa. 9:1–2; 60:1–3; cf. John 9:5). He foretold that both Zebulun and Naphtali would experience unique, sustained time with that light. This happened for Zebulun when Jesus grew up in Nazareth. It happened for Naphtali when Jesus moved from Nazareth to Capernaum.

While Matthew highlights the way this move fulfills Old Testament prophecy, the geography suggests even more. By moving to Capernaum and adopting it as his base of operations (Matt. 9:1), Jesus abandoned the isolation of Nazareth for a place connected to the world. The International Highway that linked the markets of Asia, Africa, Europe, and Arabia passed just outside Capernaum. Because news traveled with the trade caravans, this made Capernaum an international stage. What Jesus said and did in the vicinity of Capernaum gained an international audience.

Jesus's move from Nazareth to Capernaum is a bombshell. It confirms his identity as the Savior from sin and signals his passion to reach everyone with news of forgiveness—even those like us who live far from Capernaum.

🐾 What prevents you from seeing the significance of the geography in Bible passages?

🐾 In what way does Jesus's move from Nazareth to Capernaum build the bridge to the place you met Jesus?

Thank you, Jesus, for making this move. You left the inward-looking Nazareth for the outward-looking Capernaum, in part to guarantee that news of forgiveness would travel to the place where I first heard it. Now, let me do all I can to extend that news into the lives of others.

Capernaum
Mount of Beatitudes

MATTHEW 6:25–34

So do not worry, saying, "What shall we eat?" or "What shall we drink?" or "What shall we wear?" For the pagans run after all these things, and your heavenly Father knows that you need them.

Matthew 6:31–32

The Mount of Beatitudes is beautiful and quiet. It beckons for us to climb above the bustling shoreline of the Sea of Galilee, where droning buses and noisy tourists jostle for space. As early as the fourth century, Christians sat on this rise to enjoy the tranquility and contemplate Jesus's Sermon on the Mount (Matt. 5–7). This sermon and this place have a message for worriers like me.

Each of us is constrained by a set of basic needs. Our health will fade without nutrients. Our energy levels will fizzle without water. And our body will exceed temperature limits without some form of shelter—clothing at minimum. We need food, water, and clothing, but we have only partial

The parklike setting of the Church of the Beatitudes invites us to let the natural world teach us lessons about worry.

control over securing them. And if our theology ran in the same direction as the pagan world, we would find ourselves depending on false gods that do not care about us and cannot provide any of our needs. Like pagans, who run here and there after all these things, I too am tempted to worry.

There is a better way. Jesus invites us to take a stroll in the natural world. And this is where the Mount of Beatitudes shines. To be sure, it has a beautiful chapel with art and architecture that teach lessons from the Sermon on the Mount. But it is the gardens and fields preserved on the campus that immerse us in a world of flowers, grassy slopes, and wildlife.

In these verses from Matthew 6, the natural world provides the visual aids for Jesus's lesson on the topic of worry.

Birds and grasslands have the same basic needs as we do, yet they are not consumed by worry. They instinctively know what I still need to learn: the Lord who created us all cares about our needs and also controls provision. No amount of worry will improve on that.

Buildings and cities can block our view of the places that best teach this lesson, but in nature we plainly see the Father's care at work. We see it in the beautiful wildflowers and in verdant grassy fields. We hear it in the joyful songs of the birds.

The Lord liberates us from worrying about such things so that we can focus on the one thing that matters most: "Seek first his kingdom and his righteousness, and all these things will be given to you as well" (Matt. 6:33).

🌱 What things are generating worry in you right now?

🌱 Where can you go today to spend time in the natural world and experience the assurances that God is in control and cares?

Buildings and cities can be beautiful, but they teach less about worry than the natural world does. Lord, help me see your caring hand at work in all of nature. And then use what I see to eradicate the worry I feel.

Capernaum

Synagogue

> Then Jesus began to denounce the towns in which most of his miracles had been performed, because they did not repent.
>
> Matthew 11:20

After Jerusalem, Capernaum is the second most frequently mentioned urban center in the New Testament. What I love about being here is that I can stand in a fourth-century synagogue built immediately above its first-century predecessor. That means I'm looking down into the very building in which Jesus spoke and where he unleashed his divine power against human suffering. The experience is awesome, but it is also profoundly thought-provoking.

These verses from Matthew 11 are rich in geography, as Jesus mentions six different places nine times in just five verses. To understand the lesson, we must understand the geography. Jesus uses two sets of place names indicating locations that had vastly different experiences with the Lord.

The synagogue at Capernaum challenges us to consider how seriously we think about Jesus.

The first set of place names includes three towns that are all situated on the northwest side of the Sea of Galilee. Capernaum, Chorazin, and Bethsaida were Jewish towns located less than three miles apart inside the promised land. And here is the point we cannot miss: during his time on earth, Jesus did more miracles in or near these towns than in any other place.

The second set of place names includes Tyre, Sidon, and Sodom. These were Gentile places located outside the promised land, and so they had little direct revelation from the Almighty. The communication they did receive from the Lord wasn't pleasant and came in the form of scorching judgment speeches and burning sulfur raining down from the sky.

Although each set of places would face a day of reckoning, we expect the first three to know a much better experience.

But Jesus turns that expectation upside down. Capernaum, Chorazin, and Bethsaida fumbled their God-given opportunity and failed to repent. Therefore, Jesus says the day of judgment will be more bearable for the pagan cities because they will carry less regret than those so richly blessed by opportunity.

I feel the weight of that thought when I stand in the synagogue of Capernaum. Have I been as incautious as Capernaum? The people of this town who came to hear Jesus in this synagogue didn't shun him, mistreat him, or force him to leave. They just never took him seriously enough to repent of their sins and believe he was their Savior. As a result, many were banking regret that will mature when Jesus returns to this world as judge.

How are your experiences with Jesus more like those of Capernaum than those of Tyre, Sidon, and Sodom?

In what ways have you grown careless with the opportunities you've been given to walk and talk with Jesus?

This geography lesson really gives me pause, Lord. I am blessed with opportunities to hear and learn, but I realize such opportunities also come with the risk of regret. Jesus, help me to celebrate and use the time I have with you. Lead me to repent of my sin, and deepen my trust in your promises.

Chorazin
Korazim National Park

My Father's house has many rooms; if that were not so, would I
have told you that I am going there to prepare a place for you?

John 14:2

Chorazin was one of the three towns in which Jesus
did most of his miracles (Matt. 11:21–22), yet the
Gospel writers don't elaborate on even one of them.
In spite of that, this town has something special to teach us.
It offers an architectural picture Jesus seized upon to console
the disciples' troubled hearts when they became concerned
that Jesus would leave and forget about them. If you have
ever felt forgotten by God, the picture in this story is for you.

Although Jesus was speaking to them in Jerusalem, he
painted a picture that transported the disciples back to their
home life in Galilee, where people lived in *insulae* houses.
These were built not for single nuclear families but for the
large, multigenerational, extended families in which people

lived in first-century Galilee. This accounts for the dominant feature of these living compounds: a large, central courtyard. Here the extended family could cement relationships and work out problems while the kids played and communal meals were shared. This open-air courtyard gives the compound its name. *Insula* is the Latin word meaning "island." The courtyard was like an island surrounded by a sea of smaller roofed rooms.

Those smaller rooms met a second design need. Each nuclear family in the larger group needed private space for personal storage, intimacy, and sleeping. Each of the small, narrow rooms that darted off the perimeter of the insula had just one door that opened into the central courtyard, providing both connection to and privacy from the extended family.

The design of this Galilean *insula* home is a comforting reminder to those who feel forgotten by God.

We need to add one more element to this picture. Such a compound was dynamic. Each time a son within the extended family got married, another room was added to the perimeter of the insula for him and his bride. That is why places like Capernaum and Chorazin exhibit such a tangled labyrinth of wall lines in their archaeology.

Although Jesus wasn't in Galilee, his words in John 14 paint the picture of Galilean insula home life. The Father's house has many rooms. Jesus had to leave, but he was not trying to get away from the disciples. He was going to add another room to the family compound before coming back to take them to live in that new place. His departure would lead to reunion. Of all the words Jesus could have used, this image said it best.

It still does today. When we feel as if Jesus has left us all alone, when we feel the duress of separation, we can turn to this illustration. He has gone ahead to build the room in which we will live. It's the powerful picture that reminds us we are not abandoned or forgotten. "I will come back and take you to be with me that you also may be where I am" (John 14:3).

- When are you inclined to worry that Jesus has forgotten you?

- How does this image from John 14 bring you peace today?

- How could you use this word picture to comfort others?

Lord Jesus, at times I feel forgotten. But this picture reminds me that with you I am never out of sight or out of mind. Please use this to comfort me, and let me use it to comfort others who feel isolated and abandoned.

Dan

Tel Dan Nature Reserve

---
1 KINGS 12:26–30

Jeroboam thought to himself, "The kingdom will now likely revert to the house of David."

1 Kings 12:26

King Jeroboam I had a problem, and the sanctuary he built at Dan was part of his solution. But his solution became a real problem in the eyes of the Lord.

Jeroboam's problem came on the heels of a significant political firestorm and redrawing of Israel's map. The once united kingdom of Israel ruled by David and Solomon had split into two political entities, each with its own capital city and its own king.

Jeroboam was the first king of the newly formed northern kingdom of Israel. Like any new political entity, this one was fragile, and Jeroboam knew it. Many of his subjects would be traveling to visit the temple in Jerusalem, the religious capital of the Jews and the political capital of the southern kingdom of Judah. And when they did, Jeroboam knew that the familiarity of that place would lead them to agitate for reunification. He paced and fretted, feeling his new kingdom slipping through his fingers.

In response, Jeroboam developed a multipronged plan that involved building a sanctuary at Dan. He would keep his subjects from traveling to Jerusalem by tempting them with more conveniently located worship centers at Dan and Bethel. In each of these sanctuary cities, he offered a form of worship that blended veneration of Baal and the Lord. The Baal calf was joined with the Exodus story to create a new

This bronze bull (twelfth century BC) recalls the hybrid worship at Dan that shipwrecked Israel's faith.

national religion, one that was appealing to both his Baal-loving Canaanite subjects and the descendants of Abraham who still had some affinity for the Lord.

And the sanctuary cities accomplished one more purpose: they would retire the old adage "from Dan to Beersheba." Jeroboam no longer wanted to hear that expression, which had always been used to proclaim the extent of the united kingdom (Judg. 20:1; 1 Sam. 3:20). Jeroboam wanted to replace it with a geographic expression that would cement the integrity of his new kingdom: "from Dan to Bethel."

The Lord didn't celebrate the ingenuity of Jeroboam. "And this thing became a sin" (1 Kings 12:30). This was such an abomination because it perverted an accurate understanding of who God is, all in the interest of political expediency. In the end, it shipwrecked Israel's faith and charted Israel's course to exile (2 Kings 17:21–23).

The lesson lingers. The Lord is different from any pagan deity. He alone is God. Any attempt to blend away this distinction, no matter how ingenious, is an abomination that has dire consequences.

🌿 Where do you see efforts to confuse the identity of God by blending his revelation with human-made perceptions?

🌿 What can you do to prevent alternate depictions of the divine from confusing your thinking about who God is?

Father, I feel the pull to compromise. But syncretism in the interest of expediency isn't a virtue. Immerse me in your Word and in a correct understanding of your identity so that I can quickly identify and reject a blended and inaccurate picture of who you are.

Dead Sea

EZEKIEL 47:8–12

This water flows toward the eastern region and goes down into the Arabah, where it enters the Dead Sea. When it empties into the sea, the salty water there becomes fresh.

Ezekiel 47:8

The Dead Sea lives up to its name like few places do. It's *really dead* with no hope of change. So when it changes, hope stirs.

The Dead Sea is actually an inland lake at the southern end of the Jordan River. At 1,300 feet below sea level, it's the lowest place on the surface of the earth. It's also among the least inviting because it's hot. The average summer temperature is 100 degrees Fahrenheit, and it can climb as high as 125 degrees.

This uncomfortable place is also lifeless. From a distance its blue-green surface looks inviting, but the closer you get, the more disgusting it becomes. Its acrid smell and oily feel tell you there's something wrong here. This body of water is 33 to 38 percent salt by weight, which is ten times saltier

Ezekiel's vision of the Dead Sea transformed has the power to instill hope within those who feel hopeless.

than the oceans. It is too chemically fouled to support the kind of life we expect of inland lakes. It has been that way for millennia, and it's hard to imagine it being anything but dead.

Ezekiel saw it differently, though. He had a vision in which a stream of fresh water poured out from the temple in Jerusalem. As it flowed east, the stream became a deepening torrent rushing down the Kidron watershed toward the Dead Sea.

I have literally seen this happen, when the heavy rains of winter thrash and roil down torrent beds into the Dead Sea. The result is always the same: the fresh water becomes tainted by the lake's chemical stew.

But in Ezekiel's vision, the Dead Sea becomes a freshwater lake and the entire ecosystem changes. The sterile shoreline teems with all kinds of living things. The barren lake becomes filled with so many species of fish that commercial fishermen set up operations rivaling those on the Mediterranean Sea. And fruit trees that had no chance in the salt-laden soil now bear fruit every month! The Dead Sea, which could not possibly change, does.

So can we. Speaking from the Jerusalem temple campus, Jesus said, "Let anyone who is thirsty come to me and drink. Whoever believes in me, as Scripture has said, rivers of living water will flow from within them" (John 7:37–38). The gospel message of forgiveness is the stream of water that flows into people who are dead in their sins. God considers no one to be hopeless. If he can change the Dead Sea, he can change you and me.

🌱 When are you most prone to feel that you have exceeded the reach of divine forgiveness?

🌱 How can Ezekiel's vision of the Dead Sea change how you feel about yourself today?

There are times when I feel that I have sinned in a way that exceeds the reach of your forgiveness, Lord Jesus, but I know that isn't true. You are the "living water" that can change me as surely as you can make the waters of the Dead Sea sweet.

Elah Valley

Roman Road

"Do you understand what you are reading?" Philip asked.
"How can I," he said, "unless someone explains it to me?"

Acts 8:30–31

So, how did the meeting go?" That's the question we should ask every time we read a story set in the Elah Valley or any of the other Shephelah valleys. In the Old Testament, the answer was always the same: the meeting went badly for gentiles, as illustrated in the meetings between Samson and the Philistines (Judg. 14–16) or David and the Philistines (1 Sam. 17)! Would this meeting in Acts 8 be any different?

As the story opens, we meet a man bouncing along in a chariot. He is unique in many ways. He's a black African man who has a high-powered position as the superintendent of the treasury of Ethiopia (modern Sudan). He is literate, and he has little tolerance for ambiguity. Remember, he is an accountant—numbers always add up the same way.

Luke also tells us that this man is a God-fearer, a gentile who is attracted to the monotheism of the Jewish faith but who hasn't committed to full conversion and all its practices.

But most important, this man is frustrated. We hear it when he speaks. He has just come from worshiping at the temple in Jerusalem. But he had left this center of biblical learning without the answer to a question that continued to vex him, a question associated with Isaiah 53:7–8. *Was this poet speaking of himself or someone else? If someone else, then who? How can I understand unless someone explains this to me?!*

The geographical setting of the story doesn't bode well for the confused man. He had left Jerusalem and was on his

The remains of this Roman road set the stage for the story in Acts 8 that speaks about how we use our meeting places.

way to Gaza via "the desert road" that led back to Ethiopia. The most user-friendly route for a chariot descending from Jerusalem to Gaza followed the same route as the later Roman road that transited the Elah Valley in the region of the Shephelah. The Shephelah are the foothills to the Judean mountains, and their east-west valleys connect the mountain interior with the coastal plain. That made the Shephelah a meeting place of cultures and ideas.

Most importantly, it made the Shephelah the place where the stories of salvation that evolved in the mountains met the rest of the world that traveled on the coastal plain. The Lord intended the story of salvation to meet the gentile world here. But the Old Testament doesn't contain a single Shephelah story in which the meeting went as the Lord intended.

That is, until Acts 8. Philip explains the connection between Isaiah 53 and Jesus, which leads the Ethiopian to recognize Jesus as Savior. And when they come to water, this new believer receives baptism—a first for him and for the region.

God has a plan to use our "Shephelah" places as well—maybe the local coffee shop, the lunchroom at work, even our living room. These are the places we may meet people who, like the Ethiopian man, need help in finding Jesus.

🔹 What are the meeting places that the Lord uses to put you in touch with those who are confused about life and their relationship with Jesus?

🔹 In what ways could you make better use of the meeting places the Lord has provided in your life?

Lord, I know that there are many people who feel frustrated and uncertain about who you are and how you think about them. Please help me to use the places I meet them to pour the news of hope and forgiveness into their lives.

Gideon's Spring
Ma'ayan Harod National Park

JUDGES 7:1–8

The LORD said to Gideon, "With the three hundred men that
lapped I will save you and give the Midianites into your hands.
Let all the others go home."

Judges 7:7

Gideon's Spring still gurgles from the base of Mount
Gilboa in a serene park that is popular with local
Israeli families who come to camp, picnic, and
play in the water. They come to this green space in order
to relax by the spring and escape the tough questions we
all face in life.

Ironically, the Lord brought Israel here for very different
reasons—to prepare for war and to face this difficult question: Is one God enough?

Israel's stumbling answers to this question haunt every
story in the book of Judges, which is where we meet the first
generations of God's chosen people who came out of the

wilderness. These families who were settling in the promised land had no experience growing food there, so they turned to their Canaanite neighbors for a lesson in local agriculture. Some of the advice was benign. Israel learned when to expect rain and dew and how to time the planting-harvesting cycle accordingly.

Then came the insidious part: the Canaanites insisted that Israel must worship Baal, the local deity that provided the vital rain and dew. They weren't asking Israel to abandon the Lord. They were simply honoring the ancient Near Eastern maxim that one god is never enough. And Israel made the theological compromise. Even Gideon's family built a center for Baal worship in their town (Judg. 6:25–26).

This theological betrayal led to invasion, as the Lord allowed people from the adjacent eastern desert to repeatedly raid the promised land. The Midianites, Amalekites, and other eastern people groups had no interest in seizing territory, only the food that the Israelites had grown. As these hungry hordes poured into the land, they left Israel impoverished and despairing (Judg. 6:1–6).

Now the Lord had Israel's attention. And he set about using this moment to reteach them a fundamental principle that distinguished Israel from its pagan neighbors: one God is enough.

Then, as Gideon assembled the tribal soldiers for action against the invaders, the Lord began sending them home! From a tactical perspective, this was unthinkable. The armies of Israel and Midian were both similarly equipped. The one variable that a general like Gideon could control was the number of soldiers he'd lead into battle. In ancient contests like this, catastrophic loss of life was the norm, with victory

Gideon's Spring is where the Lord asked and answered this important question: Is one God enough?

going to the army that was able to absorb the greatest number of casualties. So, how did Israel's numbers stack up? As the soldiers gathered to hydrate at the spring, Gideon was outnumbered four to one (compare Judg. 7:3 with 8:10).

And that is when the Lord tells Gideon, "You have too many men" (Judg. 7:2)! The Lord instructs Gideon to keep reducing his numbers until he is left with a mere three hundred soldiers. It's with this paltry group that the Lord demonstrates his ability to save by many or by few.

I, too, am tempted to look at the numbers, whether it's the number in my bank account or the number of social media followers I have. But only one number is critical to my success and well-being: we have *one* God. I dare not underestimate his ability to save by many or by few. One God is enough when our God is the Lord.

🌿 When have you faced a challenge in life that left you questioning if God was enough?

🌿 How does Psalm 73:25–26 relate to the encouragement offered at Gideon's Spring?

Lord, I confess that when life takes a hard turn, I am tempted to look for solutions beyond you. I fear that you are not enough. Please use this time to remind me that the one God I have is enough. "Whom have I in heaven but you?"

Har Bental

The Road to Damascus

ACTS 9:1–22

Yet Saul grew more and more powerful and baffled the Jews living in Damascus by proving that Jesus is the Messiah.

Acts 9:22

Har Bental offers a panoramic view of northern Israel as well as a look into the life of a passionate man whom Jesus shaped for kingdom service. The slow rise of molten rock from the earth's mantle made Har Bental what it is today. This extinct volcano cone rises to nearly 4,000 feet above sea level and offers an unobstructed view for dozens of miles.

The first thing that seizes our attention is Mount Hermon, just ten miles to the northeast. This mountain ridge stretches for twenty-eight miles and rises to an elevation of 9,232 feet above sea level. For ancient travelers, it was a natural roadblock. They wanted nothing to do with its steep slopes and alpine snowfields, so they respectfully walked below on the road that led from Har Bental to Damascus, some forty miles away. This is the same road to Damascus that was the site of Saul's conversion.

Saul was a diligent student of the Jewish faith who learned from the best scholars in Jerusalem. He was one of those students you knew was going to be special, distinguishing himself by his abilities and his passion for Judaism. That enthusiasm shows up in the opening verses of Acts 8. Saul

The road to Damascus was the setting for a story about redirected passion.

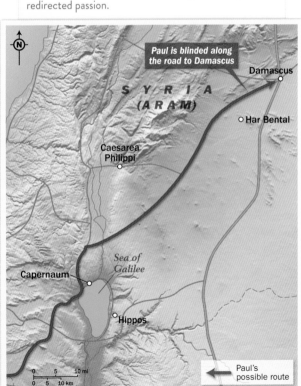

viewed the followers of Jesus as heretics, and he sought to destroy the early church by killing its leaders in Jerusalem, starting with Stephen (vv. 2–3).

By the time we get to Acts 9, Saul has turned his attention to Damascus. Apparently, Jewish believers in Jesus who lived there were talking about their Savior with Jewish pilgrims passing through on their way to Jerusalem. The very "heresy" Saul sought to drain from Jerusalem was being recharged by those coming from Damascus to the Holy City. This had to stop! And Saul was zealous enough to travel all the way to Damascus to end it.

As Saul was en route and nearing the city, Jesus appeared to him and began his conversion. And here's what I find so interesting: Jesus didn't send Saul back to Jerusalem but told him to go to Damascus! That's where the scales of misunderstanding fell from his eyes, and this persecutor of the church became a baptized member of it (Acts 9:18). But he was no ordinary member. All the passion Saul had brought to harming the church was now redirected to building it (v. 22). The very thing Saul had gone to Damascus to stop now becomes the thing he zealously pursues.

This is a story of redirected passion, and it serves as a reminder to us that passion isn't enough. Misinformed and misdirected zeal harm the church's cause. Today is the day to stop and make certain that we are not just passionate about Christ's church but that our passions are well informed and well directed.

🐝 What do you feel most passionate about when it comes to the church?

🐝 How can you be certain that those passions are well informed and well directed?

Lord Jesus, stop me in my tracks today for a passion check, just as you stopped Saul. Help me pulse with the well-informed, well-directed, post-conversion passion of Saul.

Hazor

Tel Hazor National Park

JOSHUA 11:10–11; JUDGES 4:1–3, 23–24

> At that time Joshua turned back and captured Hazor and put
> its king to the sword. (Hazor had been the head of all these
> kingdoms.)
>
> Joshua 11:10

Hazor! Its very mention struck fear in the hearts of the ancient Israelites. Compared to Jericho, Megiddo, and other city-states within Canaan, Hazor stands out.

What we know of Hazor comes from various sources, all of which emphasize its prestige and power. The city is repeatedly mentioned in ancient accounts from Egypt and Mesopotamia, which speak of it as a burgeoning economic center with the military might to defend its wealth. The archaeology from Hazor adds to the picture of its prominence. Starting around 1500 BC, Hazor stamped out an urban footprint that grew to two hundred acres and became the largest city in

The geography of Hazor made it wealthy and powerful, but not more powerful than the Lord.

the region. To see it from the ancient Israelites' perspective, realize that Hazor was six times larger than Jerusalem at the time of Solomon and twenty-five times larger than the average village in Old Testament Israel.

Its fearsome reputation and dominance grew from Hazor's unique location along the International Highway between Egypt and Mesopotamia. It was located where certain natural features severely limited people's travel options. To the west, the near-vertical Naphtali Ridge rose 2,600 feet above the city. To the east, the 30,000-acre wetland, which today is called the Huleh Basin, splayed out across the landscape so that the only realistic route led to Hazor's front door. Ancient merchants, their pack animals laden with merchandise, had no option but to stop and pay the demanded tariffs. With each passing caravan, Hazor grew richer and more powerful.

Given all that, the authors of Joshua and Judges represent Hazor with the kind of language we would expect. In comparing it with other city-states, Joshua calls it "the head of all these kingdoms" (Josh. 11:10). The book of Judges twice mentions that Hazor came into battle with nine hundred iron-enhanced chariots, a piece of military technology for which Israel had no tactical answer (Judg. 4:3, 13).

Hazor stood out in dramatic fashion from other city-states, and that raised the question: Was the Lord strong enough to give Israel victory in battle against the most dominant force in the region? Both Joshua and Judges offer an answer in two separate encounters with Hazor that they record. In both instances, Israel marshaled its forces to deliver a resounding defeat. At the time of Joshua, Hazor was "totally destroyed" and "burned" (Josh. 11:11). At the time of Judges, it was "subdued" and "destroyed" (Judg. 4:23–24).

The looming shadow of Hazor takes different names in our lives today: cancer, divorce, bankruptcy. Each one carries a powerful punch and threatens to undermine our well-being. Is the Lord strong enough to deliver the victory? A walk through the ruins of Hazor gives us the answer. Although Israel on its own had no answer for Hazor's wealth, size, and power, the Lord did. And in Hazor, we see that no opposition we face is strong enough to thwart the Lord.

🐝 Where do you see the church facing powerful opposition akin to that of Hazor?

🐝 Where do you see a force in your personal life akin to that of Hazor?

🐝 How does the story of Hazor's defeat bring you encouragement?

Lord, I have a tendency to see the opposition as being stronger than your kingdom. Please use this story from the past to help me honor the power you're ready to unleash in my present.

Hebron

Machpelah

GENESIS 23:1–20

So the field and the cave in it were deeded to Abraham by the
Hittites as a burial site.

Genesis 23:20

The exchange of property that we witness in Genesis 23 was one of the most significant real estate deals of all time.

Abraham is grieving the death of his wife. He and Sarah had been married for more than one hundred years. Together they had battled infertility and faced dysfunction within their blended family. Experiences that could have torn them apart instead deepened the bond between them. In this chapter we can feel, see, and hear the pain of their separation. In the background of Genesis 23, we hear the Hebrew word for death (*mwt*) tolling like a bell nine times. In the foreground, we watch Abraham mourn and weep (v. 3). And we listen as he agonizes over being "a foreigner and stranger" (v. 4) without any land at a time when he desperately needs it to provide a grave for Sarah. All this is further complicated by the fact that the Lord had promised to give Abraham the land of Canaan (Gen. 12:1–3, 6–7), which hadn't happened. And now Abraham acutely and personally feels the pain of that unfulfilled promise.

That's when the Lord quietly goes to work. We can't see it unless we recognize that the real estate in the Hebron basin is some of the best agricultural land in the Judean hill country. It's unthinkable that a family would sell it. And if they did, it's unimaginable they would sell it to someone outside their extended family. But the Lord leads Ephron the Hittite to sell this fertile parcel of land to Abraham, a foreigner.

The Machpelah in Hebron marks the first parcel of land that Abraham's family owned in the promised land.

This gives Abraham just what he needs. First, it provides a place to bury his beloved wife, a place that will not be contested in the future. But even more powerfully, this land deal gives Abraham hope of reunion with his bride. The Lord had firmly connected his promise of redemption and eternal life to Abraham's family and to the land he would give them. Until this moment, Abraham and Sarah had pitched their tents and pastured their animals on land owned by others. The vital element of land ownership had been missing from their story, but once the silver changes hands and the deed is delivered, Abraham legally owns part of the promised land. And for him this brings hope. This transfer of land signals that the Lord is keeping his promise to save sinners, which meant that one day Abraham would be reunited with his beloved bride.

That's how this story about death becomes a testament to life beyond death. When pangs of grief roll over us, this tomb in Hebron joins with the empty tomb of Jesus in Jerusalem to comfort us in our loss. Both speak of God's fulfilled promise to redeem sinners and his commitment to reunite us with our loved ones who have gone to be with the Lord.

🐟 Where do you find yourself in this story of Abraham and Sarah?

🐟 How does this story speak to the grief in your own life?

Death is powerful, but you are stronger, Lord. Please use this place to remind me that you make good on your promises, particularly the promise to redeem me from sin and reunite me with my loved ones.

Herodium

Herodion National Park

If you believe, you will receive whatever you ask for in prayer.

Matthew 21:22

erod the Great didn't intend for the Herodium to be the object of a faith lesson. He built this palatial complex as a wilderness watch station and entertainment venue. Jesus had other plans for it. He often taught about prayer, demonstrated it, and even gave the disciples a pattern to follow in the Lord's Prayer. But something was still missing, and the Herodium was just what Jesus needed to address it.

No, you didn't miss something. Jesus doesn't mention this luxurious mountain resort by name in this passage, but there's little doubt that when he says "this mountain" he is referring to the Herodium. As Jesus traveled over the Mount of Olives from Bethany to Jerusalem, the Herodium would have been clearly visible a little more than seven miles away.

This model of the Herodium helps us to visualize Jesus's illustration about the power of prayer.

With its five-story hall and eight-story tower, it stood out from all the surrounding terrain.

The Herodium was perfectly round in shape, and it actually had a history of being moved! As part of Herod's construction plan, workers shaved off the mountain adjacent to the building site and deposited the material around the base of the Herodium to create a 32-degree slope around the hall's perimeter. By all accounts, "this mountain" was an excellent choice for Jesus's object lesson.

The Herodium may have been an impressive piece of architecture, but the disciples weren't enamored with the place. As members of the working class, they had paid taxes for this government project, but they didn't benefit from it. They weren't invited to enjoy a meal in its lavish dining room or relax beside its massive swimming pool complete with its own island. They could only watch as social elites and dignitaries entered the complex via its glistening marble staircase. When the disciples looked upon "this mountain," they recoiled in disgust. It symbolized all that had gone wrong in society, reminding them of the Roman occupation of their land and the financial abuse of the poor.

"This mountain" needed to be moved again, and "the sea," meaning the nearby Dead Sea, was the perfect place for it. For observant Jews living in the Holy Land of Jesus's day, the Dead Sea was where they threw any pagan object they discovered. If only God would take Herod's sprawling palace and dump it in the Dead Sea where it belonged! Such a move was nice to imagine, and the disciples might dare to put this on their wish list, but it was too much for them to put on their prayer list.

Sound familiar? We also tend to artificially limit our prayer life by treating our prayer list as if it were merely a wish list. That needs to change. Jesus points in the direction of the Herodium and says, "If you believe, you will receive whatever you ask for in prayer" (Matt. 21:22). The impossible is possible: mountains can be moved.

🌿 What subjects make it to your wish list but never to your prayer list?

🌿 Why have you felt underconfident about the power of prayer?

🌿 How do you hear Jesus speaking to you today regarding your prayer life?

Lord, it's time for me to pray about my prayer life!
I confess that I often treat my prayer list like a wish
list. I hope for things to happen and change, but
I have little confidence that my prayers can move
a mountain. Please replace my uncertainty with
confidence.

Jericho
Tel eg-Sultan

JOSHUA 6:1-20

Then the Lord said to Joshua, "See, I have delivered Jericho into your hands, along with its king and its fighting men."

Joshua 6:2

The story of Jericho's fall is both engaging and entertaining, a Sunday school favorite. But it has more to offer the church than we usually harvest. Enshrined in this story are three steps to Israel's success that can bring success to the church as well.

First, Israel picked a worthy opponent. The book of Joshua tells the story of Israel conquering the land of Canaan. They engaged with strategic targets in a specific order, and Jericho was first on the list because it was vital to the rest of the plan's success. Joshua's eyes were on the larger goal of conquering the Benjamin Plateau about seventeen miles west of Jericho. This high plateau was like an ancient traffic circle for the interior crossroads of Canaan, and it was the key element in Joshua's plan to divide and conquer the cities of the interior. But to obtain the Benjamin Plateau, Joshua had to defeat Jericho first. This fortified city superintended all the roads that radiated westward from the Jordan River, and it provided the last major spring before entering the waterless Judean wilderness. By all accounts, Jericho was a relatively small outpost, but it was the first and necessary target of Israel's assault.

Second, Israel followed the Lord's unconventional battle plan. Had they followed conventional military thinking, Israel had two options: either make a frontal assault on the city or enact a siege. The first option was fast but would cost many lives. The second option would spare soldiers needed for the battles yet to come but could take months before

Jericho was secured by layers of defenses, as illustrated here. Nevertheless, the Lord had a plan for overcoming them all.

exhausting Jericho's food and water supplies. The Lord's unconventional plan spared lives and was fast. But would Israel dare to follow such an eccentric battle plan with so much at stake? Absolutely! A signature feature of this story is its repetition: The Lord laid out the plan (Josh. 6:2–5). Joshua and Israel followed the plan without changing or omitting a single detail (6:6–20).

Third, Israel awaited a miracle. Whether that miracle was a perfectly timed seismic event in this earthquake-prone region or a direct manipulation of the wall's foundation, Jericho's defenses collapsed. Israel expected it because the Lord had promised it (Josh. 6:5).

This story from the past gives the church a path into the future. Pick a worthy opponent, follow the Lord's plan, and expect a miracle. What might we accomplish as God's people if we approached a fallen world the way Joshua approached Jericho?

🐾 How do each of these steps apply to the church as it engages its mission?

🐾 Where have you seen a local church either succeed or fail in its mission because it followed or diverged from this outline?

Heavenly Father, I pray that the church of today might learn from this story from the past. Success will follow naturally when we avoid distractions and face only worthy opponents, honor your plan, unconventional as it may be, and then expect miracles. Help us be that kind of church.

Jerusalem

PSALM 132:7–14

> For the LORD has chosen Zion,
>   he has desired it for his dwelling, saying,
> "This is my resting place for ever and ever;
>   here I will sit enthroned, for I have desired it."
>   Psalm 132:13–14

Jerusalem mediates the tension between who God is and who I need him to be.

God is clearly other. He is big, powerful, and transcendent. The biblical poets and prophets often express the distance on a vertical scale, placing the Lord beyond mortal reach. He is seated on a throne in the highest heavens surrounded by his angels (Ps. 113:4–6; Isa. 6:1–4). Solomon despaired of containing him, even in his newly completed temple: "But will God really dwell on earth? The heavens, even the highest heaven, cannot contain you" (1 Kings 8:27).

But I need God to be close, and that's where Jerusalem comes in. To walk in Jerusalem is to walk beside God.

Jerusalem, as it would have looked in the time of Solomon, is a city that reveals who God is and who I need him to be.

Psalm 132 is one of the Songs of Ascent that the Israelites sang as they traveled to Jerusalem for worship. In Psalm 132, we learn that the Lord chose Jerusalem (Zion) as his own so that he could live among his people. We cannot fully explain or understand it, but here the transcendent God who cannot be contained is locally present in a unique way. The psalmist describes Jerusalem as God's "dwelling place," "footstool," and "resting place" (vv. 7–8). The Lord "desired [Zion] for his dwelling, saying, 'This is my resting place for ever and ever; here I will sit enthroned, for I have desired it'" (vv. 13–14). In Jerusalem, God was present with his people in a way that he wasn't in Israel's other towns and villages. It's no wonder people celebrated the opportunity to be in the Holy City, a place where they could encounter God in intimate fashion, pouring out their praise, their pain, and their needs.

Jerusalem is also a placeholder for what is to come. The writer of Hebrews sensed the limitations of the earthly Jerusalem: "For here we do not have an enduring city, but we are looking for the city that is to come" (Heb. 13:14). The Jerusalem of today will give way to the New Jerusalem. And just like its earthly counterpart, the heavenly Jerusalem will mediate the tension between who God is and who we need him to be. "And I heard a loud voice from the throne saying, 'Look! God's dwelling place is now among the people, and he will dwell with them'" (Rev. 21:3).

No wonder God's people come to love this city. Despite the gridlock of Jerusalem's streets, the honking horns, and the smog, Jerusalem remains the Lord's home on earth. Here he is near. What's more, it remains the one city on earth that also gives us a taste of what is to come in eternity. Jerusalem is a place we can walk beside the Lord.

🍃 When in life have you been troubled by the apparent distance of God?

🍃 What does Jerusalem have to say to you about navigating life's challenges?

Lord, you are big and powerful and transcendent. But I need you near me. Please use my visits to Jerusalem, whether in person or virtual, to remind me that you are by my side. And let me see that the Jerusalem of today is a down payment on the Jerusalem to come—a place where you will personally wipe all tears from my eyes.

Jerusalem

Bethesda Pools

JOHN 5:1–15

"Sir," the invalid replied, "I have no one to help me into the pool when the water is stirred. While I am trying to get in, someone else goes down ahead of me."

John 5:7

When we listen with a sympathetic ear, we can hear the disabled man's frustration in John 5:7. "What's the use? No one will help me!" He had given up on everyone, including God.

Jesus met this man at the Bethesda Pools in Jerusalem. We can visit the site today and see the two deep pools located near the eastern gate of the Old City. Most visitors are surprised by their size. Combined, the pools offer five thousand square feet of surface area and are much deeper than most people imagine.

At the time of Jesus, five colonnaded, covered porches offered visitors a bit of shade, one along each of the complex's four sides and one along the twenty-foot-wide divider that separated the two pools (see John 5:2). The Bethesda Pools were not a public swimming pool but a public works project designed to collect runoff water and make it available to the citizens living in that district of Jerusalem. But our attention isn't drawn by those coming to fetch water but by the disabled people who gathered here hoping to be healed. They embraced the superstition that when the water was

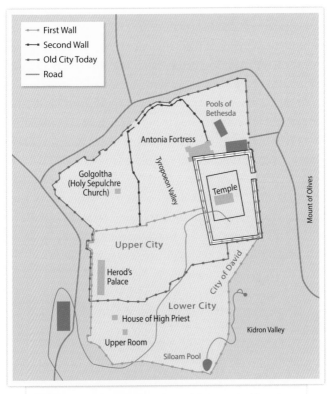

The Bethesda Pools lay just north of the temple. Here Jesus met a man who had given up on everyone, including God.

miraculously stirred, the first person into the pool would be cured.

Among them was a man who had lived with his debility for thirty-eight years. His hope for healing had all but vanished. Every day was frustrating for him, but the festivals made it worse. On those days, he saw thousands of people who had walked dozens of miles from their homes to the Holy City, while he couldn't even walk a few steps to the pool.

Realize that at this spot he was a mere one hundred yards from the temple, the very place where the Lord had promised to hear the prayers of his people. But this man had chosen to bet on superstition rather than the Almighty, and that remains the case even when Jesus shows up.

In the Gospels, we typically see people with disabilities seeking out Jesus and calling to him for help. But in this story, Jesus sees the man and asks him if he wants to get well. His answer is stunning: "Sure, I could use your help. You can help me get into the water."

Unfazed by the man's disillusionment, Jesus offers what he hasn't requested. Jesus directs him to pick up his mat and walk. And he does! As we watch him walk away, he leaves this lesson for us in his wake: we may give up on God, but Jesus never gives up on us.

🎵 What experience in life left you uncertain of God's interest or ability to help?

🎵 How does this story help you speak to a person who feels alone and abandoned by everyone, including God?

Lord Jesus, I'm so grateful that you don't ignore me when I give up on you. Please help me today. I trust you can help where I cannot help myself. Please provide what I most need to find peace and well-being today.

Jerusalem

Broad Wall

---

2 CHRONICLES 32:1–8

Be strong and courageous. Do not be afraid or discouraged because of the king of Assyria and the vast army with him, for there is a greater power with us than with him.

2 Chronicles 32:7

I've looked at the Broad Wall from many angles. It's unattractive from them all. Those who stop for a look (and many don't) quickly move on to more interesting sites in the Holy City. But when we know its story, this unassuming wall teaches one of the most powerful lessons Jerusalem has to offer, a lesson for those overwhelmed by their circumstances.

The wall's builder, King Hezekiah, was an aggressive reformer who reversed the horrendous policies of his predecessor, King Ahaz. Ahaz had fostered trust in all the wrong places, believing that his country's survival depended on building a strong alliance with the Assyrian Empire (2 Chron. 28:16). And he sought to secure that relationship with Assyria by adopting their worship practices and encouraging the worship of pagan gods, even going so far as importing them into the Lord's temple (2 Kings 16:10–14; 2 Chron. 28:2–4, 22–24). Hezekiah worked to disassemble every one of these policies that robbed the temple and the Lord of their due respect (2 Chron. 29:1–11; 31:1).

King Hezekiah's religious reforms also had ramifications for national security, because they shattered the alliance his father had made with Assyria. Hezekiah knew the Assyrian army would soon be on the march, so he prepared Jerusalem for the inevitable siege through a number of public works projects. He strengthened existing defensive walls (2 Chron. 32:5) and expanded the city's defensive perimeter from 32 acres to 125 acres by adding walls that enclosed two neighboring hills to the west. This is where we find what remains of the Broad Wall.

You may be curious about its name. This section of the new wall transited through a dip in the terrain, so it was built higher to offset the topography. To keep the wall stable, this higher section also had to be built wider, hence its name. This surviving section of Hezekiah's building efforts shows not just where this wall was positioned but how aggressively Hezekiah worked to create the additional space Jerusalem needed to accommodate refugees fleeing the Assyrian invasions. It quietly but powerfully teaches us that when faced with impending challenges, Hezekiah did what he could.

When the Assyrian army arrived, Hezekiah gave his citizens a pep talk. But instead of encouraging them to trust in the things he had done, he urged them to look confidently

The foundation of the Broad Wall demonstrates just how much Hezekiah could do. Yet he encouraged his citizens to trust the One who could do more.

toward the Lord, the "greater power with us" who is ready "to help us and to fight our battles" (2 Chron. 32:7–8).

Here is a model to follow. When faced with unparalleled challenges, Hezekiah did what he could and then trusted the One who could do more. The Broad Wall reminds us to do the same.

❧ What circumstances have you faced or are you facing now that have left you feeling overwhelmed?

❧ What can you do to foster trust in the One who can do more?

Lord, I feel overwhelmed—as overwhelmed as Israel must have felt watching the powerful army of Assyria advancing against them. Help me to follow the lead of Hezekiah. May I do all I can, and then may I trust you, the One who can do more.

Jerusalem

Church of the Holy Sepulchre

JOHN 19:17–20:18

> Carrying his own cross, he went out to the place of the Skull
> (which in Aramaic is called Golgotha). There they crucified
> him. . . . At the place where Jesus was crucified, there was a
> garden, and in the garden a new tomb, in which no one had
> ever been laid.
>
> John 19:17–18, 41

For followers of Jesus, the Church of the Holy Sepulchre is the most significant site in the Holy Land. It
commemorates Jesus's crucifixion, which paid our
sin debt, and his resurrection, which confirmed the Father's
acceptance of the payment. Some heroic acts can safely remain in the world of make-believe. This one cannot.

John carefully marks the spot for us in his Gospel. He
gives us the name of the place: Skull or Calvary. He also
notes that Jesus was buried in a new tomb located "at the
place where Jesus was crucified" (19:41). With this language,

This mosaic from the entry to the Church of the Holy Sepulchre captures the moment the price was paid for our salvation.

John brings the two events together and marks the location with a name so that his first readers could visit it.

And visit it they did. By the close of the first century AD, the place with the gruesome name had already become a holy site for pilgrimage and worship by followers of Jesus. But it was the Roman emperor Hadrian who built the first permanent structure here. Hadrian's goal was to make Jerusalem a pagan city, so he changed the city's name to *Aelia Capitolina* to echo the pagan worship of Rome (the Capitoline Hill in Rome hosted multiple temples, including one dedicated to the worship of Jupiter). He also sought to extinguish non-Roman religious sites, including those associated with Jesus. Therefore, in AD 135, Hadrian covered Calvary with a stone platform on which he established a temple dedicated to Venus.

Ironically, his attempts to extinguish the location's significance helped to preserve it. The children of those who had witnessed Jesus's crucifixion and resurrection watched the platform being built. And when Helena, the mother of the first Christian emperor, Constantine, came to Jerusalem looking for holy sites, believers pointed her to the platform that covered Calvary. In the years that followed, the pagan sanctuary was replaced by the first church to be built on the site. Dedicated in AD 335, the Church of the Holy Sepulchre has occupied the spot ever since.

We need to be certain that Jesus "was delivered over to death for our sins and was raised to life for our justification" (Rom. 4:25) because our eternity depends on it. To be sure, this is first and foremost a matter of faith. But the evidence represented by the Church of the Holy Sepulchre corroborates the story. The curse of sin has been lifted and death has been defeated.

🌿 Why would the Lord secure the spot of Jesus's death and resurrection with such a strong memory and such enduring evidence?

🌿 How would/will a visit to the church strengthen your faith?

Lord, I need forgiveness and hope of life beyond death. Thank you for affirming Christ's death, burial, and resurrection through the enduring witness of your Word and the corroboration offered by the Church of the Holy Sepulchre. Please use my visit, whether in person or virtual, to confirm my confidence in these events that changed my eternal destiny.

Jerusalem

*City of David
Observation Tower*

**1 KINGS 11:7–8; 2 KINGS 25:8–11;
2 CHRONICLES 36:15–19**

But they mocked God's messengers, despised his words and
scoffed at his prophets until the wrath of the LORD was aroused
against his people and there was no remedy.

2 Chronicles 36:16

The 360-degree view from the observation tower at
the City of David is breathtaking as well as story-
filled. Our reward for climbing dozens of steps to
the top is an unobstructed panorama of Old Testament Jerusalem and a set of stories that put the Holy City on a collision
course with destruction.

Looking to the north, we can see the sprawling platform
on which Solomon built Jerusalem's first temple. Although
the temple itself is gone, we can imagine how it soared above

Israel's capital city. Other nations also had worship centers in their capitals, but these pagan plazas always contained multiple temples designed for worship of many deities. Jerusalem had just one temple because the Lord revealed to ancient Israel that God is one (Deut. 6:4). Jerusalem's single temple stood as an enduring sermon in stone.

To the east we can see the two-mile-long ridge of the Mount of Olives rising some three hundred feet above the site of Solomon's temple. Here we find another of King Solomon's building projects, but one with a darker side. The highest portion of the Mount of Olives hosted multiple temples he built and dedicated to the deities worshiped by his foreign wives (1 Kings 11:7–8). As we look first at the Temple Mount

The destruction of these buildings on the east side of the City of David, which date to the sixth century BC, illustrates the consequences of unrepented sin.

and then at the Mount of Olives, we feel the tension. One view asserts God is one; the other holds that there are many gods. Something had to give. And eventually it did.

We can see what happened by looking south and allowing our gaze to settle below on the ruins of homes dating to the sixth century BC. Among the rubble, archaeologists have uncovered clay seals baked hard by intense heat, charred wooden beams, and Babylonian arrowheads strewn among the toppled walls. These all testify to the sudden and catastrophic destruction of Jerusalem by the invading Babylonian army.

These three views from the City of David Tower merge to illustrate an important lesson. The Lord is patient with sinners, calling them to repent. But when the Holy City repeatedly scoffed at the prophets who called the people to return to the Lord, time ran out. "The wrath of the LORD was aroused against his people and there was no remedy" (2 Chron. 36:16). The lesson still applies today: unrepented sin comes with consequences.

❧ How is the idea of sin softened in our society?

❧ How might society's softened view of sin impact our relationship with the Lord?

❧ Where do you find this lesson from Jerusalem calling you to change?

Heavenly Father, you are a righteous God who abhors sin and rebellion, including mine. Help me to see my sin for the real threat it is, lead me to repent of my sin, and spare me from the consequences of my poor choices.

Jerusalem

City of David Royal Palace

---

2 SAMUEL 5:6–12; 7:11–16

David then took up residence in the fortress and called it the
City of David.

2 Samuel 5:9

The LORD declares to you that the LORD himself will establish
a house for you.

2 Samuel 7:11

The palace of David in the City of David explains a
lot. It explains why the biblical authors and poets
mention the Holy City more than one thousand
times. It explains why modern Israelis feel so passionate
about Jerusalem and why Christian pilgrims fall in love with
the place.

Let's start with Jerusalem's role in Israel's political history.
David came to the throne following a civil war that lasted six
and a half years. He desperately needed a capital city that

ticked three boxes: it had to be centrally located, secure from attack, and neutral during the civil war.

Jebus met all three criteria. But taking this ten-acre ridge from the Jebusites was no easy task since it was naturally defended by deep valleys on three sides. So David directed a special forces unit to clandestinely enter the city through its underground water system—an operation so daring that it multiplies the mystique of Jerusalem's founding story.

Once captured, David's capital city needed a public building to function as the iconic symbol of the state, much like the White House does today. Enter David's royal palace. The current excavation at the City of David corroborates three key details from the Bible's description of this palace fortress: it was built on top of a stepped-stone retaining wall; it was massive in size, with a footprint thirty times larger than ordinary homes of that era; and it was adorned with Phoenician-style design flourishes (2 Sam. 5:9, 11). By all

A Phoenician capital like this one was discovered below the palace of David, a place that links the promised Savior to both David and Jerusalem.

accounts, this palace stood out and bonded Jerusalem with Israel's political history.

But it did more than that. The palace also became part of the spiritual legacy of the city. To see this, we need to understand the wordplay around the Hebrew word *byt* in 2 Samuel 7. This elastic term appears fifteen times in this chapter. David was living in his *byt*, the royal palace. Disturbed by the fact that the ark of the covenant resided in a tent, he determined to build a *byt*, a stone temple, for the Lord. The Lord countered by telling David that he was going to build a *byt*, a dynastic family, for David.

Then came the lightning bolt: the promised Savior would be a member of David's own *byt* or household. This revelation linked the plan of salvation not only with David's family but also with Jerusalem.

It's no wonder that Christians have fallen in love with this place. Not only was Jerusalem the political capital of Israel, but it also remains at the heart of the story that brings us salvation. This is where the great King David lived and where David's greater Son would die on the cross to bring eternal life to us all. And for that reason, Jerusalem remains what it has been since the days of David: a city of hope.

🌿 How has this story about David's palace in Jerusalem changed the way you will respond to mention of Jerusalem in the Bible?

🌿 What makes Jerusalem a place of hope and comfort for you?

Lord, I so often feel overwhelmed by life and the power sin has over me. Please use Jerusalem, as you have through the centuries, to restore hope when I'm feeling hopeless.

Jerusalem

Herod's Palace

When Pilate heard this, he brought Jesus out and sat down
on the judge's seat at a place known as the Stone Pavement
(which in Aramaic is Gabbatha).

John 19:13

E verything about Herod's palace was meant to impress
visitors and intimidate the locals. This is where Jesus's civil trial took place before Pilate (John 18:28;
19:13). Yet in the case of Jesus, it failed to have its intended
effect of terrifying the person on trial.

It's difficult to pick out the design and nature of Herod's
palace from what's left of the structure. So we need to recon-
struct our impressions based on the ruins we can see and the
descriptions we find from first-century writers. This luxury
palace sprawled between the modern Joffa Gate and the
southwestern corner of the modern Old City Walls. While
most people of Jesus's day lived in homes with only one or
two rooms, this palace had hundreds of rooms. The parklike

This model of Herod's palace in Jerusalem shows its grandeur, which was meant to impress visitors and intimidate the locals.

center of the complex was open to the sky and featured groves of trees, flowing streams, and walking paths lined with ornate works of art. It was home to the elite, a place the first-century historian Josephus called "wondrous beyond words."

By the time of Jesus's trial, Herod the Great was dead. Rome ruled the land with governors who used Herod's palace as their residence while in Jerusalem. They used it to intimidate the locals. As governor, Pontius Pilate was both the political face of Rome and the empire's chief judicial officer in the region. In his court, there was no jury. Pilate heard the evidence and handed down the verdict, which could only be overturned on appeal before the emperor in Rome.

To make matters worse, Pilate was politically compromised. News of Pilate's insensitivity, cruelty, and poor leadership had severely eroded the Roman senate's confidence in him. Pilate's final years in office were marred by erratic verdicts, which were increasingly subject to bribes and the influence of the aristocratic Jewish priests.

This is the intimidating and unstable setting Jesus enters for his civil trial. He is quickly confined in an unfamiliar building, separated from his associates, surrounded by Roman soldiers, and accused of a capital crime—all as he stands before an unpredictable judge. Yet it isn't Jesus but the judge who seems intimidated. Jesus's calm demeanor and confident responses recall the language of Psalm 2. When the political forces of the world band together against the Lord's anointed, "the One enthroned in heaven laughs; the Lord scoffs at them" (v. 4).

Many places and people in this world intimidate us. But they don't intimidate Jesus. And we see it here. The very place so carefully designed to intimidate is instead intimidated by the King of Kings and Lord of Lords.

*How does the place of Jesus's trial before Pilate impact your understanding of Jesus's experiences there?

*How can this story of Jesus help you when you feel intimidated?

Lord, help me appreciate what your trial and its location say about you. Anyone else would have been intimidated. You were not. Help me find confidence in the control you have over the most powerful things in life so that I can feel more confident when facing situations that otherwise intimidate me.

Jerusalem

Jerusalem Archaeological Park, Southern Steps

—— LUKE 2:40–52 ——

Didn't you know I had to be in my Father's house?

Luke 2:49

This story is about a place Jesus had to be. He refers to it as "my Father's house," an expression used to refer not just to the temple proper but to the Temple Mount campus that sprawled over more than thirty-six acres. In the first century, a visit to this campus began with a climb up the so-called Southern Steps that now reside within Jerusalem Archaeological Park.

The design of these steps involved careful thought. Today the width of a stair's tread is constrained by building codes that demand strict uniformity, but that wasn't the case with the Southern Steps. The individual steps vary in width, making it impossible to climb them without giving careful thought

These steps were the main entry for the temple in Jerusalem, a place Jesus said he "had to be."

to the effort as well as to where those steps are taking you. In addition, their southern exposure offered passive solar heating, making this a favorite gathering spot for the senior scholars of Jerusalem and their students during the winter months. In traditional Jewish writings, these were known as the "Teaching Steps."

And that helps us understand the story at the end of Luke 2. The only story we have from Jesus's teenage years is framed with these words: "he was filled with wisdom" (v. 40) and "Jesus grew in wisdom" (v. 52). Luke doubles down on this theme by filling the intervening verses with language that repeatedly references learning. Jesus assumes the posture of a student. He was "sitting among the teachers, listening to them and asking them questions" (v. 46). This is a story that involves "understanding" and "answers" (v. 47), searching and knowing (vv. 48–49). That's what this story is about and why Jesus had to be here.

But wait a minute! Doesn't Jesus know everything? As true God, yes. That is why he regularly shared insights that exceeded the bounds of human knowledge. But to fully replicate our experience as mortals, Jesus limited his access to all the knowledge available to him so that he could learn just like we do. Jesus's education started at home but soon shifted to the synagogue of Nazareth when his questions surpassed the answers Mary and Joseph could provide. And when the local rabbi also came up short, Jesus turned to the senior scholars of Jerusalem. That's why Jesus stayed in Jerusalem when his parents left for Nazareth. He had to be *here* to get the answers Nazareth could not offer.

This story, as much as any other, helps us appreciate the full humanity of Jesus. He could not merely simulate the human experience. To be our substitute, he had to be fully human. And to be fully human meant that he needed to learn the history of his people and the role he would play in delivering the world from sin. Jesus had to be more than human to redeem us from sin, but he could be no less. That is why Jesus had to be here at the Southern Steps, to grow in wisdom.

🌿 What prevents you from thinking more often and appreciatively about the humanity of Jesus?

🌿 How does the fact that Jesus understands the entire human experience firsthand change the way you pray to him in a time of need?

Lord Jesus, thank you for daring to be what we are. Today help me appreciate your humanity, something I often overlook. You had all the experiences in life that I've had, including going to school and learning. Help me approach you in prayer as someone who knows what I'm facing.

Jerusalem

*Jerusalem Archaeological Park,
Southern Steps*

ACTS 2

> And you will receive the gift of the Holy Spirit.
>
> Acts 2:38

The Southern Steps also hosted the great day of Pentecost, a day we get a new answer to the question "Where is God when I need him?"

The events of Pentecost began in a Jerusalem home (Acts 2:1–2), but the narrow confines of a residential quarter couldn't contain all that happened next. There are several reasons I believe the event moved to the Southern Steps. The first has to do with the large number of diverse participants in the story. During the Jewish high festivals, pilgrims scattered throughout the Holy City to find lodging and food. But when it was time for worship, they converged here at the temple's main public entry. The Southern Steps would have provided the open space the narrative demands to accommodate the large, diverse crowd we meet in the story (2:5–11).

Second, the Southern Steps provided Peter with an acoustic advantage. At the top of the steps soars the south retaining wall of the Temple Mount. Peter's voice could reach thousands with the acoustic assistance of this wall.

And finally, this location set the stage for the baptisms of those who accepted Peter's message. Adjacent to the Southern Steps was a public ritual bath that visitors to the temple used to prepare themselves for worship. This was likely the place where some of the three thousand who believed received baptism that day (Acts 2:41).

The location of the Pentecost story is worth pursuing because it brings us to the subject of divine presence and the

This model depicts the southern entry to the temple, the most likely setting for the story of Pentecost in Acts 2.

theological crisis triggered by Jesus's ascension. In the Old Testament, the temple was where the Lord made his presence known in a special way (2 Chron. 7:1–12). Here God's people came before him to confess their sins and receive forgiveness. Here they poured out their pain and knew the Lord was beside them.

When Jesus came to earth, things got even better, as God incarnate was present throughout the Holy Land, bringing aid to the hurting and encouragement to those overrun by life's challenges. But following Jesus's ascension from the Mount of Olives, just to the east of where the first Pentecost took place, the question arose: Where is God now when I need him?

The answer is given on the Southern Steps of the temple, the site of Peter's Pentecost sermon just ten days after Jesus's ascension recorded in Acts 1:9–11. After calling his listeners to repent and be baptized for the forgiveness of sins, Peter declares, "And you will receive the gift of the Holy Spirit" (Acts 2:38). This gift is the indwelling presence of God in every believer (Rom. 8:9–10), which makes our bodies temples of the Holy Spirit (1 Cor. 6:19).

This means Pentecost opens a new chapter in the story of God's presence. He doesn't live beyond the farthest galaxies. He isn't limited to the temple in Jerusalem or even to the Holy Land. When we need him, he's right there with us because he lives within us.

🌱 When in your life have you felt a need to be as close to the Lord as possible?

🌱 How has understanding the location of Pentecost changed your understanding of the divine presence?

Lord, I need you. I need the forgiveness you offer, and I need to know you are present when my life takes a hard turn. Thank you for being with me and within me.

Jerusalem
Kidron Valley Overlook

MATTHEW 24:1–3

> As Jesus was sitting on the Mount of Olives, the disciples came
> to him privately. "Tell us," they said, "when will this happen, and
> what will be the sign of your coming and of the end of the age?"
> Matthew 24:3

Washing machines, cars, buildings—they all stop working or fall into ruin. Does anything last? Jesus's answer in Matthew 24 echoes through the view from the Kidron Valley Overlook.

As Jesus and the disciples were walking up the ridge on the far side of the valley, they glanced back at Jerusalem and the disciples commented on the apparent permanence of the temple complex (Matt. 24:1; Mark 13:1). Herod the Great had expanded the temple's worship plaza to thirty-six acres, making it the largest in the world. Today we catch only a glimpse of what it looked like, and even that is impressive.

To achieve a level plaza across undulating terrain, Herod built retaining walls that soared 160 feet above the Kidron

The Kidron Valley sprawls at the foot of the Mount of Olives, a setting that causes us to think about what endures.

Valley floor. This involved the shaping and placing of massive stone blocks. The largest of these is 43 feet long by 15 feet wide and weighs about 570 tons. Just one stone is impressive; combined they are extraordinary. The disciples would have seen glistening, ornate buildings that rose another eighteen stories atop the level plaza held up by these retaining walls. It's no wonder they were impressed by the seeming permanence of it all (Matt. 24:1). But Jesus had a different take: within forty years, the whole thing would lie in ruins (24:2).

Does anything in life last? Yes, it does. To see it, Jesus moves our eyes from the temple to the local topography. When the Old Testament prophets spoke about the final judgment and the end of time, they used geographical language that puts us in this exact location. Joel mentions the Kidron Valley ("Valley of Jehoshaphat"; Joel 3:2, 12–16) and

Zechariah mentions the Mount of Olives (Zech. 14:4) as the places where the final judgment will occur. No wonder Jesus gave his longest discourse on the end times here!

As we look across the Kidron Valley and meditate on Jesus's words, we discover what endures. It's not the stunning architecture of Jerusalem. It's not even life itself. On the day when the Son of Man comes in his glory and sits on the throne of judgment in this very place, he will say, "Come, you who are blessed by my Father; take your inheritance, the kingdom prepared for you since the creation of the world" (Matt. 25:34).

Jesus came to secure the not-guilty verdict for sinners. He made sure that when he comes again, we will endure.

🌿 What places or events in life have caused you to reflect on the end of life?

🌿 How does the setting for the final judgment bring encouragement to you today?

Lord Jesus, thank you for taking me on this walk with you to a place that stirs thoughts of what is to come. Help me think and live differently today. I see so many things around me that will not last for eternity, but I know that I will. Fill me with the hope of the life to come.

Jerusalem

Nebi Samuel National Park

Surely the LORD was fighting for Israel!
Joshua 10:14

Nebi Samuel National Park safeguards the traditional tomb of the prophet Samuel and offers a front-row seat to one of the most consequential battles recorded in the Bible—the battle for the Benjamin Plateau. This story in Joshua 10 highlights how the Lord responds when we come to a significant intersection in life.

The Benjamin Plateau lies just north of and five hundred feet below our viewing platform at the traditional tomb of Samuel. A look around the horizon makes it clear that nothing in Israel's interior is flat!

Even today the promised land isn't a place that you can travel wherever you want to; you can only go where the mountainous terrain yields enough to permit passage. In

The Benjamin Plateau was a travel intersection, and it's a place in Scripture where we meet people in transition. Nothing ends here. But how things end up starts here.

ancient times, this meant north-south travelers had to stick close to continuous ridgelines, and east-west travelers had to look for breaks in the mountainous façade, such as a high plateau. What makes the Benjamin Plateau unique is that it offers both: it is a high plateau that intersects Israel's north-south watershed ridge. Like a modern traffic circle, it gathered travelers from many places before sending them off in new directions. It's a major geographical intersection, and the stories that it hosts are of people whose lives are in transition.

That's what makes the geography such a vital character in Joshua 10. It is a story ripe with tension. Joshua's soldiers have just made an all-night, forced march to the battlefield and are more ready for rest than for fighting. When they arrive, for the first time they face an army mustered from multiple city-states. On top of these two challenges, the battle is for control of the Benjamin Plateau.

Victory here is vital to all that follows. If successful, Israel will collapse communication and coordination between the remaining cities of the interior. The outcome of Israel's divide-and-conquer strategy is on the line.

All that makes us lean in to see what will happen next. If our attention gets stuck on the poetic insert of verses 12–13, we may feel some frustration, because Joshua's enigmatic language about celestial bodies has been interpreted in a variety of ways. The prose portion of Joshua 10 is clearer and puts the focus where it belongs: on the Lord's actions. He throws the enemy into confusion (v. 10). He hurls large hailstones on them as they flee (v. 11). He gives Israel the victory (v. 12).

And therein lies the enduring lesson. Just like Joshua and the Israelites, when we come to a significant intersection in life, we can know the Lord will be with us and guide the turns we need to make. Nothing ends here. But the way things end up starts here.

🌱 Give examples of times your life came to an intersection.

🌱 Why are intersections like these accompanied by so much tension?

🌱 How can this story help you when your life comes to such an intersection?

Lord, you know how challenging life can be. Please assure me of your presence as I enter the round-abouts of life. Guide me through the intersection, and send me confidently down the road you have chosen for me to take.

Jerusalem

Old City Walls

"Is not my word like fire," declares the LORD, "and like a hammer that breaks a rock in pieces?"

Jeremiah 23:29

The Old City Walls are an iconic part of the Holy City. Stretching for 2.7 miles, they encircle and embrace the historic quarters of Jerusalem. Even though they were built in the sixteenth century, long after the time of the New Testament, they help us envision walled cities of the past and deliver insights into the language of Jeremiah 23.

By standing close to the wall and craning our necks upward, we get a sense of just how massive these defenses were and how much effort it took to put them in place. Every block of stone had to be quarried, transported, shaped, and levered into position. Towns and villages couldn't afford defensive walls; cities couldn't afford to be without them. When enemy

Jerusalem's Old City Walls (sixteenth century AD) help us understand both the purpose of ancient walls and the power of God's Word.

soldiers showed up, the locals would hide behind what the
prophet Nahum calls a "protective shield" (Nah. 2:5) and
wait for the enemy to leave.

The enemy's early departure could be motivated by a
variety of circumstances. They might run out of food and
water before the city's stockpile gave out. But it was just as
likely for a siege to break because the attackers needed to
return to defend their homeland against attack or because
the soldier-farmers had to return to plant next year's crops.

That's why an attacking army might employ siege tactics
designed to speed up the process. The poetry of Jeremiah
23:29 seizes on two of those tactics. The "rock" in this verse
is likely an allusion to the stones of a city wall. The "hammer"
and "fire" are two ways of attacking the wall and compro-
mising its integrity. The hammer represents the battering

ram slammed against the wall in a bid to cause its collapse. Considering how durable this type of limestone is, this was no easy task. Take a close look at the Old City Walls and you are looking at stone that erodes at the leisurely rate of only one centimeter every thousand years!

Fire was another tool a besieging army used against a solid limestone wall. To understand this, we need to begin with the fact that limestone breathes. When this porous stone inhales, moisture enters and becomes trapped in its passageways. This collected moisture doesn't harm the wall until it's heated. By building an intense fire at the base of the wall, the attacking army turned the trapped moisture into steam that expanded and shattered the rock.

Early in the nineteenth century, Edward Bulwer-Lytton observed that "the pen is mightier than the sword." Long before that, Jeremiah observed that the Word of God is mightier than any force that could be brought against an ancient city's defensive walls. I dare not underestimate what it can do in my life.

🌿 What insight from this lesson proved most helpful to you as a reader of God's Word?

🌿 What other metaphors are used in the Bible to express the power of God's Word?

You have so much to say to us, Lord. But because the Bible looks like any other book, there's the risk I will give it less attention. It is not like any other book, though. Motivate me to be a better listener by keeping this image in mind: your Word lands with the force of a hammer and fire.

Jerusalem

Pool of Siloam

"Go," he told him, "wash in the Pool of Siloam" (this word means "Sent"). So the man went and washed, and came home seeing.

John 9:7

This Jerusalem story set at the Pool of Siloam challenges us to revisit how we think about and interact with those who have disabilities.

When Jesus's disciples saw the man born blind, they treated him like a nameless object lesson: "Rabbi, who sinned, this man or his parents, that he was born blind?" (John 9:2). Their words betray a common misperception later echoed by the Pharisees (9:34) that moral failings were the cause of physical disabilities. Consequently, people who were disabled were shunned by the respectable crowd and were not welcome to worship at the temple.

When Jesus looked at this man, he saw something quite different. He approached him, spat on the ground, and made a poultice of mud and spittle that he put on the man's eyes. Once that's done, we expect Jesus to say to the man, "Open your eyes and tell me what you see." Instead—and *although the man still couldn't see*—Jesus directed him to go to the Pool of Siloam and wash off the mud. What is this about?

The Pool of Siloam is located in the southernmost sector of Jerusalem and at its lowest elevation. Here it collected water from the Gihon Spring via a tunnel system constructed at the close of the eighth century BC. The blind man would have approached a renovated three-quarter-acre pool that had three sets of stairs, enabling visitors to walk down and into the water as its level changed.

People went to the Pool of Siloam for two reasons. First, it was a water source for those living in the southern part of the Holy City. Second, and more important to the story in John 9, it was a ritual purification bath.

These steps lead down to the Siloam Pool, where Jesus showed how he regards those with disabilities.

In the first century AD, those going to worship at the temple first had to fully immerse themselves in water. Smaller ritual baths called *mikvah* are found throughout Jerusalem, but the Pool of Siloam met all the necessary criteria for a bathing station and could accommodate hundreds of people at one time. So when Jesus sent the blind man to the Pool of Siloam, he was directing him to a place where he could prepare for worship.

And therein lies the significance. Even before the man regained his sight, Jesus regarded him as someone who had every right to go to the temple and worship. And in doing so, he subverted the mistaken notion that people with disabilities were somehow undeserving of God's love and unfit for worship.

It sends the same message to us. Those who have disabilities are persons fully valued by the Lord.

🌸 What messages does society send to people with disabilities that signal they are less than whole?

🌸 How can the church work to subvert those messages and show that the Lord values people who have disabilities?

Lord Jesus, please make me aware of times when I diminish those with disabilities by my thoughts or actions. And as the church, please help us do what you did for this blind man. Love demands no less.

Jerusalem

Temple Mount

Woe to you, teachers of the law and Pharisees, you hypocrites!

Matthew 23:15

Jesus unleashed a chapter-long torrent of criticism against Israel's religious teachers while he was on their home turf: the Temple Mount. The location was part of what prompted the tirade.

The Temple Mount as it appears today wasn't part of the first temple's plan. When King Solomon built the first temple, he laid its foundation on a hill that is no longer visible today. This location elevated the building to a deserved place of prominence, but it also created a problem. Because the terrain fell sharply away from this hill, particularly to the south, it limited the number of people who could gather for worship.

The solution was to reshape the topography. By the time of Jesus, retaining walls and subsurface arches joined to support a level thirty-six-acre worship plaza that boasted colonnaded porches and open courtyards where people could gather.

Jesus spent considerable time here during his final week in Jerusalem (Matt. 21:12, 23), and he was frustrated with what he saw. The Temple Mount called for a person to be on their best behavior. After all, it meant standing as close as you could get on earth to the throne of the Almighty. The attitudes and behaviors of the teachers of the law and Pharisees didn't match the place. This led Jesus to deliver a powerful warning shaped around the refrain "You hypocrites!" This is strong language that echoes six times throughout this chapter.

A hypocrite is a pious pretender, someone who feigns to be someone they aren't. And Jesus saw no shortage of examples on the Temple Mount. He saw it in the Pharisees' use of worship aids (Matt. 23:5). Phylacteries, or tefillin, are leather boxes that are bound to the right arm and forehead and contain portions of Scripture as a reminder to keep God's Word close to one's head and heart (Deut. 6:8). Zizith are the tassels woven into the bottom of a garment that sweep back and forth and remind the wearer to obey Torah (Num. 15:38).

On the Temple Mount, tefillin and zizith were used by many as worship aids. There is nothing wrong with that. But in the case of Israel's religious teachers, they had become symbols of hypocrisy. These men supersized their tefillin and zizith to elevate themselves above others. Such hubris was inappropriate in any place, but especially in the presence of God.

This kind of hypocrisy has no place among God's people, especially among the religious teachers and particularly in a

Tefillin are leather boxes that contain portions of Scripture and are worn on a person's forehead and right arm. These worship aids became the subject of Jesus's sermon on hypocrisy.

sacred space. What a powerful lesson this chapter leaves in its wake. Nearly every time the Gospels record Jesus speaking on the topic of hypocrisy, he is doing so in connection with worship. While Jesus is generally disgusted by hypocrisy, he finds it thoroughly repulsive in sacred space.

🌿 Where have you observed hypocrisy in religious contexts?

🌿 How did that hypocrisy make you feel?

🌿 How can we work to keep hypocrisy out of our lives in general and sacred places in particular?

Lord Jesus, clearly you are repulsed by hypocrisy. This behavior is such an affront to you in sacred places because it draws attention away from you. Please help me identify it quickly and drive it entirely from my life.

Jerusalem

Tower of Siloam

LUKE 13:1–8

Or those eighteen who died when the tower in Siloam fell on them—do you think they were more guilty than all the others living in Jerusalem? I tell you, no! But unless you repent, you too will all perish.

Luke 13:4–5

I've stood by the Pool of Siloam many times but have never heard anyone mention this tower. In the time of Jesus, however, the tower and the tragedy that happened there would have been all that people talked about.

The Siloam tower appears to have been part of Herod the Great's renovation of the water collection and storage system on Jerusalem's south side. Here the Central and Kidron Valleys converge at the base of a steeply sided ridge called the City of David. To stand here is to stand at the lowest point in Jerusalem, making it the perfect place for a reservoir. This is where we find the Pool of Siloam, best known as the place where Jesus healed the man born blind (John 9).

There's no definitive archaeological evidence for the location of this tower, but we can sense the need for such a fortification when we stand beside the pool. Jerusalem's natural defenses are poorest here. The low elevation that makes this the perfect place for a reservoir also makes the walls that protect it highly accessible to enemy attack. And since the pool of water just on the other side of those walls could sustain the city if it came under siege, it made for an appealing target. No place in Jerusalem feels more vulnerable than the area around the Pool of Siloam.

But initial efforts to build a defensive tower near the pool turned tragic. We don't know exactly why the tower collapsed. It could've been due to poor preparation of the ground on which the foundation was laid. It could have been because

Jesus used the collapse of the Siloam tower, pictured in this mural, as an illustration to warn against having a casual attitude toward sin.

the stone selected for the foundation courses wasn't strong enough to support the weight. It could've been unstable because the base was too small for the height of the tower. Whatever the error in calculation, the tragic outcome was unmistakable: eighteen people died when the tower suddenly collapsed.

Jesus doesn't address the shoddy construction practices, but he does address the false assumption associated with the collapse. Some of his listeners presumed that the eighteen who lost their lives in this accident must have sinned more seriously than others who were spared. Such grading of culpability minimized the impact of sin in one's life, and that diminished the felt need to repent. Jesus wasn't having it: "I tell you, no! But unless you repent, you too will all perish" (Luke 13:5).

Sin is sin. If we underestimate its power, undervalue its consequences, or underrate our culpability, we face far worse prospects than the tragedy that befell those who died when the Siloam tower fell.

🦋 What most easily leads you to diminish the significance of sin in your life?

🦋 How can you correct your mistaken notions about the power of sin in your life?

I confess that I have diminished my own sin by comparing myself with others. Lord, please help me take my sin seriously, repent, and turn to you for forgiveness so that I can avoid the peril of eternal separation from you.

Jerusalem

Upper Room

For who is greater, the one who is at the table or the one who serves?

Luke 22:27

The upper room hosted several landmark events of the New Testament. According to Cyril, the bishop of Jerusalem (AD 348), this first-century room witnessed the first celebration of the Lord's Supper, the first post-resurrection appearance of Jesus to the disciples, and the start of Pentecost.

But it also hosted the less frequently discussed dustup over social rank that broke out among the disciples.

Two things provoked this dispute: the disciples' unwarranted adoption of Gentile-Roman thinking and the table they used for dinner. In Roman culture, people were obsessed with rank and climbing the social ladder. Some of this rubbed off on the disciples, infecting them with an unhealthy interest in prestige. Jesus said they were acting like kings who maintained

The triclinium in the upper room provoked a dustup among the disciples over social status.

their position by force or benefactors who used benevolent acts to garner the esteem of others (Luke 22:24–25).

Although such ill-advised Roman thinking was behind the disciples' dispute, its more immediate cause was the table in the room. Mark tells us the upper room was "furnished" (Mark 14:15). That means it came with a *triclinium*. This was not a table with chairs as pictured in da Vinci's famous painting *The Last Supper*. Rather, a triclinium was a table that rose only a few inches above the floor. Those dining at the table reclined around three sides of it (Luke 22:14). In Roman culture, social rank determined where each dinner guest took their place. If we look at the table from above, the long side at the top was reserved for the host and special guests. Moving clockwise, the adjacent shorter side was reserved for those of higher social rank. The third side, opposite the host and special guests, was for those of lower rank. Those reclining on the lower-rank wing were expected to serve the others, and so "a dispute also arose among them as to which of them was considered to be greatest" (22:24).

Jesus broke up the unhealthy argument by stating that those in his kingdom don't seek to climb the social ladder but to descend it: "The greatest among you should be like the youngest, and the one who rules like the one who serves" (Luke 22:26). The words didn't land with the force intended. The disciples shuffled to their places around the triclinium, some out of necessity to the lower-status wing, but no one was willing to take on the lowly task of washing the others' feet. So during the meal, Jesus quietly rose from his place, removed his outer garment, wrapped a towel around his waist, and did what the disciples thought was beneath them.

And that is the powerful upper room lesson meant to stop us from the unhealthy pursuit of prestige in society or within the church today.

🌱 Where have you observed jockeying for positions of importance, both in society and in the church?

🌱 How can you live out Jesus's example of humble service?

Lord Jesus, we are prone to think more highly of ourselves than we ought. I confess that I have presumed and even demanded preferential treatment. Forgive me for my hubris, and help me live out the life of service set before me.

Jerusalem

Western Wall

---

2 CHRONICLES 6:12–42

As for the foreigner who does not belong to your people Israel but has come from a distant land because of your great name and your mighty hand and your outstretched arm—when they come and pray toward this temple, then hear from heaven, your dwelling place. Do whatever the foreigner asks of you.

2 Chronicles 6:32–33

If stones could speak, the stones of the Western Wall would have stories to tell. Today they offer a lesson on prayer.

The massive stone blocks at the base of the Western Wall aren't building stones connected with the temple proper. They're the remains of a west-facing retaining wall that held up the thirty-six-acre platform around the temple.

No matter what time of the day or night you visit, there are always dozens if not hundreds of Orthodox Jewish men and women praying before the massive stones of *HaKotel* ("The Wall"). They're so invested in this old wall because

The Western Wall in Jerusalem is a favorite place to pray and to leave written prayers tucked in the wall.

it's the sole architectural element that survived the Roman destruction of the temple campus in AD 70. Consequently, it became and remains an open-air synagogue where worshipers can be as close as possible to the place where the temple once stood but where the Dome of the Rock now stands.

At this wall, men and women gather alone or in small groups, touching the blocks of stone and swaying in cadence with their prayers. Before they leave, some tuck their printed prayers into the cracks of the aging wall, leaving their personal petitions before the Almighty.

What reason would a Christian have for doing this? It isn't because we believe this is the only place the Lord hears our prayers. Solomon acknowledged as much when he offered the dedication prayer at the first temple. All creation cannot contain the Almighty, much less a modest building

(2 Chron. 6:18). But that doesn't mean praying at a heritage site lacks value.

At the Western Wall, we remember the Lord's long-standing interest in listening to the prayers of his people. Solomon's lengthy prayer reminds us that the Lord is concerned about all things that impact our personal well-being, including social disruptions, environmental catastrophes, and guilt over sin.

What's more, Solomon observed that the Lord is interested not only in the prayers of his chosen people but also in the prayers of "the foreigner" like me who comes to this place to pray (2 Chron. 6:32–33). So, while the Western Wall isn't the only place to pray, it can be a meaningful one—a place that has long awaited our visit.

🌿 Is there a heritage site that is a particularly meaningful place for you to pray?

🌿 How does Solomon's prayer at the temple encourage you to compose your prayer life?

Heavenly Father, I want to pray more often and more thoughtfully. I know you are always more eager to hear than I am to pray. Help me fix that. Fill my days with conversations with you.

Jerusalem

Wohl Archaeological Museum

> But Peter had to wait outside at the door.
> John 18:16

The luxurious homes preserved in the Wohl Archaeological Museum give us a look into the lives of the Sadducees, Jerusalem's aristocratic priests. But they also illustrate the way in which first-century social and architectural settings contributed to Peter's denials of Jesus.

After Jesus's arrest, Peter and John followed behind until they arrived at the home of Caiaphas. Peter had to wait outside. Unlike John, he was not known by the household staff. In time, John secured Peter's entry to the house, but it seems the two became separated, because John's name doesn't reappear in the story of Peter's denials. Alone in an unfamiliar setting, Peter quickly found himself immersed in a social and architectural nightmare.

This palatial house in Jerusalem's Upper City is like the residence of Caiaphas. Its layout set the stage for Peter's denials.

Peter made two miscalculations about the social context. First, he presumed anonymity. But his identity as a Galilean was easily recognizable by his rough mannerisms and his distinctive accent (Matt. 26:73). This connected Peter to Jesus, but it did not reveal him as part of Jesus's inner circle. Then Peter stepped closer to the fire to warm himself. The flickering flames illuminated his face enough so that he was recognized by a relative of Malchus, the man whose ear Peter had cut off when Jesus was arrested (John 18:10). This person had seen Peter with Jesus in the garden. Peter was outed.

What Peter does next is influenced, in part, by the home's architecture. We get a sense of what that house was like by visiting the Wohl Archaeological Museum, which preserves palatial first-century homes from Jerusalem's Upper City. These were the homes in which Israel's religious elite lived.

We cannot be certain that one of these was the house of Caiaphas, but we can be certain Caiaphas lived in a house like this.

So let's look around and set our story in this kind of house. The home of Caiaphas sprawled much like the museum's largest home, which has an area topping six thousand square feet. Like the Wohl homes, it was ornate, with mosaic tile floors and walls painted with frescoes that simulated marble with floral motifs.

The home of Caiaphas was also complicated. The Wohl villas have reception halls, private bathrooms, dining areas, and bedrooms all connected by a maze of hallways. And at the heart of all these rooms was an open-air courtyard where a fire could be built. We don't see Peter wandering the hallways of Caiaphas's house but standing in such a courtyard warming himself by the fire. I suspect Peter looked for a way out once people began to recognize him, and I can only imagine how panicked and trapped he felt in this web of unfamiliar passageways. At that point his denials multiplied.

Being in an unfamiliar place where he was unknown doesn't excuse Peter's denials. But by entering the house of Caiaphas, Peter put himself in a social and architectural context that left him vulnerable. And that serves as a powerful reminder to us. We can't control when temptations come, but we can avoid settings in which temptations are harder to manage.

🦗 When have you found yourself in a context
   that made it more difficult for you to handle a
   temptation?

🦗 How does Peter's decision to enter the home impact
   how you think about the relationship of physical and
   social context to temptation in your own life?

Lord, you know that I can make bad choices about
where I choose to be. Please use this episode from the
life of Peter to make me think more carefully about
those choices and how social and physical context
impact my ability to manage temptation.

Jezreel

Tel Jezreel

— 1 KINGS 21:1–16; 2 KINGS 9:6–37 —

Yesterday I saw the blood of Naboth and the blood of his sons, declares the LORD, and I will surely make you pay for it on this plot of ground, declares the LORD.

2 Kings 9:26

The city of Jezreel witnessed three macabre stories, all related to one another. The climactic moment of each is connected to Naboth's vineyard.

In the ninth century BC, King Ahab built a sprawling fortress with four defensive towers at Jezreel. This fortress functioned in two ways. The first was economic. Ahab had diverted the trade routes so that merchants bringing wool from Moab and spices and aromatics from Arabia to market in Israel had to travel right past Jezreel. The towers were perfectly positioned to keep an eye on the caravans and assure the flow of tariffs into Israel's coffers.

This slope below Tel Jezreel was the site of Naboth's vineyard, which teaches a lesson about divine justice.

The second role of Jezreel had to do with national security. This fort guarded the road that led south from the Jezreel Valley to Israel's capital city, Samaria. That meant it functioned as an early warning station to help secure the capital against attack. From both economic and national security perspectives, Jezreel was more important than all the cities of the northern kingdom except Samaria.

However, the Bible's mention of Jezreel isn't related to either of these roles but to a mundane desire of Israel's king. King Ahab wanted a local vineyard that belonged to Naboth and offered to purchase it from him. When Naboth refused, Ahab sulked, and his nefarious wife, Jezebel, began to scheme. Jezebel was a Phoenician princess who lived by the moral code of her Baal-worshiping family. She quickly hatched a plan to have Naboth executed for a crime he didn't commit. Ahab joined in the infamy by seizing Naboth's vineyard as his own.

But that's not the last we hear of this matter. Naboth's vineyard became the setting for the Lord's response to such wickedness. His reaction came about more slowly than we might expect, but when it did happen, it was swift. The Lord appointed Jehu, an Israelite field commander, to address the injustice perpetrated by Ahab and Jezebel. As Jehu drove his chariot in the direction of Jezreel with the reckless abandon that distinguished him, Joram the son of Ahab, who then ruled Israel, left the fort and met him at Naboth's vineyard.

And this was where the arrow of divine justice met Joram. As Joram took his last breaths, his body was thrown on the plot of ground his parents had stolen from Naboth (2 Kings 9:21, 25–26). Jezebel was next. She had the good sense to remain inside the fortress but failed to anticipate the betrayal of her attendants. When Jehu arrived in Jezreel and called out, "Who is on my side? Who?," they threw Jezebel out of the window (9:32–33). Jehu's chariot horses trampled her before dogs dragged her body into Naboth's vineyard. What wasn't devoured fertilized the soil (9:10, 36–37).

It's disturbing to watch social injustice go unchecked. But the vineyard of Naboth reminds us that even when God's justice is delayed, its execution is certain.

- When have you been upset by the Lord's apparent lack of response to an act of social injustice?

- How does this story's persistent return to the vineyard impact the way you think about God's response to social injustice?

Father, there are times when I have been upset with you because I thought you didn't care about acts of social injustice I had seen. Please use this story to remind me that delivery of divine justice is certain even when it is delayed.

Joppa

Modern Joffa

> But Jonah ran away from the LORD and headed for Tarshish. He
> went down to Joppa, where he found a ship bound for that port.
>
> Jonah 1:3

As soon as you step into the historic quarter of Joffa (the modern name for Joppa), the feel of Israel changes. The frenetic pace of city life slows as you stroll among the art installations, galleries, and restaurants. If you continue walking among the bobbing boats in the harbor, engulfed by the smell of the sea, it's all but certain that the Mediterranean's gentle breeze will summon you to a moment of personal reflection. This wasn't Jonah's experience, however.

You might be surprised to learn that the book of Jonah puts greater emphasis on geography than on its signature "great fish." By my count, there are thirty-two references to location in its modest forty-seven verses, and the first place mentioned sets the stage for the rest.

The Lord called Jonah to preach in Nineveh, the ancient capital of the Assyrian Empire located within modern Mosul, Iraq. In Jonah's day, Nineveh was huge, covering some three hundred acres. And it was mean-spirited. During the late eighth century BC, the armies of Assyria repeatedly assaulted the promised land. They were bent on cruel conquest, and Jonah's homeland paid the price again and again.

This helps us understand Jonah's response when the Lord called him to preach in Nineveh: he headed for Joppa, a harbor town filled with fishermen and sailors. It's hard to imagine a place more different from Jonah's hometown of Gath Hepher, which was a farm community tucked high on

The modern harbor at Joffa is a place for quiet reflection, which is something Jonah did not do when he came here.

a mountain ridge. But Joppa offered something Gath Hepher did not: ships that sailed to the western side of the Mediterranean Sea. If Jonah could reach Tarshish, he would be more than 2,300 miles from Nineveh! Geographically, Jonah's response to the Lord's call was a resounding and unmistakable "No way!"

Jonah charted this course from Joppa because he saw Nineveh differently than the Lord did. Jonah viewed the Assyrian Empire as the dreaded other. And at that particular time in history, the empire was being challenged for a change by a combination of foreign invasion, famine, and earthquake. The last thing Jonah wanted to do was mount an aid campaign of any kind.

By contrast, the Lord saw the people in Nineveh for what they were: spiritually immature children who needed to know who God was and how he thought about them (Jon. 4:11).

Joppa offered Jonah the chance to stop, see things from the Lord's perspective, and reverse course. Unfortunately, he did none of the above. But we can. The Lord gives us places like Joppa too. Places to pause and reflect on our call to mission when we feel like escaping from it.

🍃 Who is your Nineveh—that is, the off-putting person the Lord is calling you to evangelize?

🍃 Where is your Joppa—a place the Lord stopped you for a moment of reflection, a place to defeat your doubts?

Lord, when I hear you calling me to mission in places filled with off-putting people, I feel like running the other way. Please stop me at the Joppa seashore to think again. Help me to see the mission before me as you do.

Jordan River

Qasr al-Yahud

> Then Jesus came from Galilee to the Jordan to be baptized
> by John.
>
> Matthew 3:13

This popular baptism site at the Jordan River witnessed a monumental shift in Jesus's life. Every time I stand here, I reflect on transitions in my own life.

We don't know much about Jesus's early years in Nazareth, but we know things had to change. The private had to give way to the public, the quiet to the pressing noise of crowds, the congenial to the contested. The Jordan River is where the transition began.

Although the Gospel writers give brief accounts, this story evolved over many days. We don't sense the passage of time unless we look carefully at the geography. Jesus left Galilee and traveled to the Jordan River at Bethany beyond Jordan

This Jordan River site remains a popular location for baptisms and is a good place to reflect on transitions in life.

(Matt. 3:13; John 1:28). Best evidence puts this event at or near Qasr al-Yahud, on the Jordan River just north of the Dead Sea. This means Jesus's trip from Galilee to Bethany beyond Jordan didn't take hours but days—travel days that provided space for thoughtful reflection on the change about to occur.

Once Jesus arrived, the location also invited reflection on change. I cannot think of another location in the Holy Land that has witnessed so many significant personal transitions.

After Moses passed into eternity on the ridge above, Joshua transitioned into his role as Israel's new leader here at the river's edge (Josh. 1:1–2).

Here at this ford, Israel transitioned from their time in the wilderness into the promised land (Josh. 3–4).

Here Elijah struck and divided the Jordan River just before he was carried to heaven in a whirlwind. Then Elisha also divided the river, recrossed it, and succeeded Elijah as the Lord's prophet (2 Kings 2:1–14).

The Old Testament prophet Malachi stirred hope with God's promise of the coming of a new Elijah (Mal. 4:5–6), a prophecy fulfilled by John the Baptist (Matt. 17:11–13). So we shouldn't be surprised to find this new Elijah baptizing in the same location where the first Elijah boarded a fiery chariot to heaven.

If there is any place in the promised land that has witnessed major transitions and lends itself to careful thought about changes we face in our own lives, this is it. And that fact likely played a role in Jesus's coming here to be baptized by John, a water rite that joined with the geography to mark the moment of grand transition into his public ministry.

As I dip my hand into the water and let it run through my fingers, I'm reminded how much change I have experienced in life. Such changes can be unsettling at best, terrifying at worst. Yet every one of those transitions, like others that occurred at this Jordan River site, was meant for my good and the good of God's kingdom.

Change is inevitable. Change is unsettling. But change calibrates us for better kingdom service.

🌿 How do you prefer to go through times of transition?

🌿 How might Jesus's baptism site change the way you understand times of transition?

Lord Jesus, I like things to stay the same, but I know that isn't realistic. Please help me to see my transitions in life the way you do, and use them to increase my contribution to your kingdom.

Judah's Hill Country
The Jerusalem Forest

Those who trust in the LORD are like Mount Zion,
    which cannot be shaken but endures forever.
As the mountains surround Jerusalem,
    so the LORD surrounds his people
    both now and forevermore.

Psalm 125:1–2

T he Jerusalem Forest is a restored, pine-filled land-scape that offers a sense of how Judah's hill country smelled, looked, felt, and functioned in Bible times. That makes it the ideal place to reflect on the language of Psalm 125. This inspired song seizes on the geographic reali-ties as one walks to Jerusalem through this region—a walk that is meant to prepare the heart for worship. Psalm and landscape join hands to reveal how God thinks about us.

The psalmist begins by declaring, "Those who trust in the LORD are like Mount Zion," the city of Jerusalem. How so? First, we are secure from harm. When it comes to location, Jerusalem has a problem: the core of the city sits in a topographic bowl. If an invading army reached the outskirts, they could set up camp on the higher ridges that loom over the city and threaten the residents from above. But getting close to Jerusalem was no easy task. The mountains of Judah's hill country guarded the western approach. For fifteen miles, a set of steep north-south ridges repelled anyone trying to attack Zion from the coast. Just as this protective shield surrounded Jerusalem, so the Lord surrounds his people.

Second, like the Holy City, we "cannot be shaken." The Jordan River valley to the east of Jerusalem is the meeting place for two tectonic plates that grind against each other. When they get stuck and that tension breaks, it causes earth-

A walk in the Jerusalem Forest of Judah's hill country brings Psalm 125 to life.

quakes of significant magnitude. Their impact is easily traced in the archaeological record of devastated cities up and down the valley. But when we move west of the rift to Jerusalem, the possibility of catastrophic shaking diminishes significantly. Jerusalem, like those who trust in the Lord, is unshaken.

Third, our security will last forever. To see the truth of this in the psalm, we need to do some geology. The mountains of Judah's hill country are composed of durable Cenomanian limestone, in which silica and iron combine to resist change. These mountain ridges erode at the leisurely rate of just one centimeter every thousand years. From a human perspective, these mountains never change. The psalmist captures this sense of permanence in verses 1–2 with the phrases "endures forever" and "now and forevermore."

A forest walk can be restorative. A walk in the Jerusalem Forest while meditating on Psalm 125 revitalizes the soul. The Lord promises that we will be like Zion: a city forever secure and unshaken.

🍃 What is currently causing you to feel unsafe and unstable in life?

🍃 What is most comforting to you today in the geographic imagery of this psalm?

Heavenly Father, you know how my life is being rocked by uncertainty and threats. Please calm my heart with the language of this psalm in which you promise to secure and stabilize my life like you do for Zion.

Judean Wilderness
En Gedi Nature Reserve

1 SAMUEL 24:1–22

"You are more righteous than I," he said. "You have treated me well, but I have treated you badly."

1 Samuel 24:17

E n Gedi is a welcome oasis in the dry and forbidding world of the Judean wilderness. This unique place is the setting for a Bible story that shows how a season in the wilderness can produce a powerful faith witness.

The meteoric rise in David's popularity following his victory over Goliath fueled a powerful jealousy in King Saul. The sitting king attempted to take the life of the future king on seven different occasions. With only a step between him and death (1 Sam. 20:3), David fled into the wilderness, a place familiar to him from his days as a Bethlehem shepherd. It was short on resources but long on hiding places. Here David repeatedly outmaneuvered his pursuers.

That is, until the moment he came to En Gedi. Saul obtained intel that David and his men were at the spring getting

The Nubian ibex gave En Gedi its name. Here David demonstrated the power of our faith witness.

water. This allowed Saul to catch David by surprise. Rather than fleeing down one of the dry wilderness canyons as they had done so often, David and his men dived into a cave. They were out of sight, but now they were trapped, outnumbered five to one, hoping against hope they would go undetected.

This situation sets up David's powerful faith witness. Saul needed to relieve himself and entered the very cave in which David and his men were hiding. He was isolated, distracted, and vulnerable. But rather than taking Saul's life, David neatly sliced off a corner of the robe Saul had set aside. He was unwilling to kill the Lord's anointed, even though Saul's death was the path that led out of the wilderness and onto the throne.

Then David did something even more spiritually courageous. After Saul exited, David stepped to the mouth of the cave and chided Saul for his lack of character while waving the severed portion of Saul's robe above his head. Unthinkably, David had given away his hiding place. We shudder to think what will happen next.

But Saul's response isn't the one we expect. Instead of sending his soldiers to seize David and the others who were with him in the cave, Saul acknowledged David's superior character and conceded David's right to assume Israel's throne. Saul's heart yielded before David's powerful faith witness.

During a wilderness season, we are prone to focus on how it impacts us. This En Gedi story challenges us to think of how such a season can impact others. As difficulties increase our faith, they enhance our testimony. Others will be watching. The Lord may use our faith witness, matured through a season in the wilderness, to transform the hearts of those whom we least expect to change.

🦗 How are you prone to respond when the Lord allows your life to sink into a season of wilderness?

🦗 When have you been impressed, even changed, by the faith witness of someone in a wilderness season?

Lord, I confess I have responded badly when I've gone through wilderness seasons. Forgive me for my bitterness, anger, and despair. Please use such times to grow my trust in you and to deliver a powerful witness to others.

Judean Wilderness

Masada

The LORD is my shepherd, I lack nothing.

Psalm 23:1

The view east from the top of Masada captures the rugged austerity of the Judean wilderness that provides the setting for Psalm 23. When we read this iconic poem in this setting, we'll hear it as we've never heard it before.

The word *wilderness* doesn't appear in Psalm 23, but the psalmist signals this is its setting by ascribing the poem to David, a shepherd from Bethlehem. When grain was growing in the local farm fields, Bethlehem shepherds would take their flocks here to the western edge of the Judean wilderness. The winter rains brought a flourish of green to at least some portions of this dry land, signaling the start of a shepherd's weeks in the wilderness.

David invites us to stand beside him and consider the view from the perspective of his flock. It lacks *everything*. Sheep and goats need to graze up to seven hours a day to survive. But as the winter weeks pass, green grasslands are out of sight and hard to find because wilderness pastures quickly retreat into isolated topographic pockets where better shade means less evaporation.

The wilderness also lacks water. The few springs and pools that exist here are just as hard to find as green grass. That's a problem for the flock, which requires watering twice a day.

Added to that, the wilderness lacks safety. Predators and hazardous terrain make it a place fraught with danger that only increased when a member of the flock strayed or when

Pasture in the Judean wilderness is short-lived and impossible to find without the shepherd's leading.

the sun set. As we stand beside David and look at the wilderness from the livestock's point of view, it isn't the place that lacks nothing but rather the place that lacks everything!

So how do we account for the language of abundance in Psalm 23? The shepherd. In the psalm's six verses, the Lord as our shepherd is referenced thirteen times. This shepherd knows where to find the isolated wilderness pastures. He knows where to find the secluded water resources. He knows how to move the flock safely through hazardous terrain and away from predators. He's the one who retrieves wandering sheep. And he's the one who takes the animals home when darkness increases the danger.

The shepherd changes the wilderness from the place that lacks everything to the place that lacks nothing.

That's why this psalm speaks so powerfully into our lives during wilderness seasons. At those moments, the view lacks all the things we need—certain provision and safety. But Psalm 23 lifts our eyes from the wilderness to the Shepherd who leads us to what we cannot see. When our eyes are fixed on him, the view that lacks everything suddenly lacks nothing.

🐾 When you are in a wilderness season, what makes you feel in need?

🐾 How does the wilderness setting of Psalm 23 change the way you hear and apply this psalm to your own wilderness seasons?

Dear Shepherd, you know what a wilderness season can do to my sense of certainty and confidence. I want to feel certainty even in my most uncertain circumstances. Please turn my eyes away from the austerity of the wilderness to all you offer. Confirm for me that I lack nothing even at those times when I appear to lack everything.

Kursi

Kursi National Park

MARK 7:31–8:13

I have compassion for these people.

Mark 8:2

Early European Christians who traveled to the Holy Land saw something special in Kursi. To be sure, the western shore of the Sea of Galilee is bursting with stories from the ministry of Jesus. But these Christians chose to build the largest of their Galilean religious compounds here on the east side of the lake. What did they find so compelling about this shoreline? The two feeding miracles answer that question.

The feedings of the four thousand and the five thousand are nearly identical stories with many details in common: Thousands of people gathered to hear Jesus speak. The crowd was so intent on listening that they outstayed their food supply. Jesus took a small amount of food and miraculously multiplied it so that everyone ate their fill. After the meal, the disciples collected basketfuls of leftovers. With all those similarities between the two feeding miracles, the differences can be easily missed.

But it's in the differences that we discover the meaningfulness. Jesus did these miracles in two different places for two different ethnic groups. The feeding of the five thousand took place on the northwest side of the Sea of Galilee. This part of the lakeshore was home to observant Jews, and a road used by Jewish pilgrims en route to Jerusalem passed through there. Both the location of this feeding miracle and the twelve baskets collected at the end mark the participants as Jewish.

The feeding of the four thousand took place in the Decapolis (Mark 7:31), on the east side of the Sea of Galilee

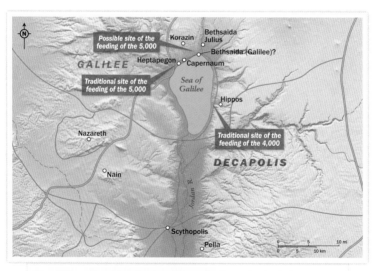

The different locations for Jesus's two feeding miracles help us understand that these miracles were not just about food but also about the reach of forgiveness.

near Kursi. It was the cultural and religious foil to the western side of the lake. The Decapolis was a gentile region filled with pagan culture. Jesus didn't shun them but invited four thousand gentile households to enjoy a meal with him—a fact reinforced by the seven baskets collected (see Deut. 7:1).

When we put these two feeding miracles side by side, it becomes clear that they're about more than food. They're also about the offer of forgiveness. Jesus did nearly identical miracles in two different places for two different ethnic groups to demonstrate that the kingdom of God doesn't discriminate. God's goodwill extends to everyone, no matter which side of the lake you call home.

And that's why Kursi was warmly cherished by the first European Christians in the Holy Land and why those of us who are gentiles find the place so compelling. It's a story of Jesus caring for people like you and me. In the end, it doesn't matter who we are or which side of the lake we live on. The geography of forgiveness extends to all of us.

🍃 In what other ways did Jesus say or demonstrate that the kingdom of God has a broader ethnic reach than some imagined?

🍃 In what ways are we prone to artificially reduce the size of God's kingdom to include only people who are like us?

Lord Jesus, I'm so grateful that your compassion and forgiveness aren't limited by social, ethnic, or cultural barriers but reach all the way to me. Now let me be an agent in making sure that the geography of forgiveness reaches as far as you intend.

Lachish

Tel Lachish National Park

Israel has forgotten their Maker
and built palaces;
Judah has fortified many towns.
But I will send fire on their cities
that will consume their fortresses.

Hosea 8:14

Lachish offers one of the best opportunities we have to examine the relationship between a Bible event and archaeology. What's more, it's one of the best places in the Holy Land to see the consequences of misplaced trust.

At the close of the tenth century BC, King Rehoboam of Judah sought to secure Jerusalem from attack by building a series of fortresses on the natural routes that led to the capital city. Lachish was one of these (2 Chron. 11:5–12).

By the close of the eighth century BC, King Hezekiah had further developed Lachish, making it second in size and

The ferocity of the Assyrian attack on Lachish is captured in this relief from the seventh century BC.

importance only to Jerusalem. During his reign, the city grew to be 150 acres surrounded by a wall twenty feet thick. The ramp and gatehouse that secured the entry are the largest to be discovered in Israel from the Old Testament era. Put all this together and Lachish illustrates what mortals were capable of doing to protect themselves from invaders.

The biblical poets and prophets had no problem with the construction of such daunting defenses, but they rose to object when they saw Israel putting more trust in what they had made than in what the Lord could do. In all eras and no matter what technology was available, God was to be

Israel's primary defense (Ps. 18:2). "Some trust in chariots and some in horses, but we trust in the name of the LORD our God" (20:7).

Hosea saw the trust of Judah flagging and warned of its consequences (Hos. 8:14). Because Israel undervalued the Lord, he would allow fortifications like Lachish to crumble.

We see that sad outcome in the archaeology at Lachish. Late in the eighth century BC, the Assyrians attacked and built a massive siege ramp against the city's southern wall. It was 246 feet wide by 200 feet long and required 19,000 tons of material.

Although the ramp has eroded over the centuries, what remains is still impressive. Archaeologists have also found an ancient written report from Assyria, the Annals of Sennacherib, in which the Assyrian king boasts that he captured forty-six of Hezekiah's fortified cities, including Lachish, effectively trapping Hezekiah in Jerusalem like "a bird in a cage." And in the entrance hall to Sennacherib's throne room in Nineveh was carved a wall relief seventy feet long depicting the defeat of Lachish in some detail. All this archaeology corresponds with the way the event is recorded in the Bible (2 Kings 18:13–16).

Listen carefully and you will hear that God is still speaking through the story and the ruins of Lachish. The Lord summons us to trust him more than we trust our retirement savings or health care plans. He calls us to trust him more than the things we construct to make our lives easier and safer. And Lachish is a reminder of what he may allow to happen to our "fortifications" if we trust what they can do more than what the Lord can do.

🍃 What "fortifications" have you put in place to secure your future well-being?

🍃 How does this story from Lachish challenge you to recalibrate your trust in the things you are able to do to secure your well-being?

Lord, I want to fully rely on you in all circum-stances. Help me make wise choices about how I prepare myself to meet life's challenges, but help me anchor my ultimate trust in you.

Magdala

Magdala Tourist Center

You are the salt of the earth.

Matthew 5:13

Bible readers likely know Magdala as the hometown of Mary Magdalene (Luke 8:2). But those who lived near the Sea of Galilee in Jesus's day knew Magdala as a salty place.

Salt had a variety of uses in Bible times, but two were most prominent: as a seasoning to improve the taste of food and as a preservative for meat. Refrigeration as we know it didn't exist in Bible times, so butchered meat had to be eaten quickly before it spoiled. The only alternative was salting. The bacteria that degrades unrefrigerated meat requires a moist environment to thrive. Salt removed most of the moisture, increasing the time meat could be safely stored and eaten.

What then led Jesus to mention salt in the Sermon on the Mount?

The Dead Sea was the primary source of salt in this part of the world, but it was out of sight, some sixty-five miles to the south of where Jesus was preaching in Galilee. Magdala was not. Here salt was rubbed into the fish harvested on the Sea of Galilee to preserve it, and the town's two names highlight this commercial enterprise. *Magdala* is the Arabic word for "tower," likely referring to a tower for drying fish. The town's Greek name, Tarichaea, means "place for processing fish." Within the ruins of Magdala we find further evidence of its connection to the fishing industry. On the shoreline, we can still make out the breakwater (230 feet long and 20 feet wide) where fishermen docked their boats to sell their catch. In the town's market, archaeologists discovered three hundred fishing weights used to anchor the base of nets and forty plastered fish tanks for holding fish prior to salting. Magdala was a salty place.

Jesus looked for the same trait in his disciples. In a world that had lost its way, they were a preserving agent much like salt in Magdala.

Salt harvested from the Dead Sea was used to process fish in Magdala, leading Jesus to speak about how we can be "the salt of the earth."

But there was a risk they could lose their saltiness. You see, salt didn't exist in the refined grains we know today. It came from the Dead Sea in chunks that contained both pure salt and other impurities. By striking a chunk on a hard surface, the fish processors broke off the salt they needed. But in time, the chunk was more impurity than salt. It was then useless and would be cast aside on the town's walkways.

How salty are we? Like he did for the disciples, Jesus has given us insights that can preserve a dying world. But to be of value, we must guard against losing our capacity to make a difference among those we meet in this world who don't know Jesus. Our actions and words matter. "You are the salt of the earth. But if the salt loses its saltiness, how can it be made salty again? It is no longer good for anything, except to be thrown out and trampled underfoot" (Matt. 5:13).

🌿 What knowledge do believers in Jesus have that the world desperately needs in order to be preserved?

🌿 What threatens to erode our uniqueness and thereby damage our effectiveness as Christians giving witness in the world?

Lord Jesus, please use me like the people of Magdala used salt. Let me be an agent that preserves the well-being of the world. And please help me combat the erosion that would damage my witness.

Megiddo

Tel Megiddo National Park

---

2 CHRONICLES 35:20–24

Josiah, however, would not turn away from him, but disguised himself to engage him in battle. He would not listen to what Necho had said at God's command but went to fight him on the plain of Megiddo.

2 Chronicles 35:22

The news from Megiddo was unimaginable: King Josiah, the reformer who worked tirelessly to clean up the worship of ancient Israel, was dead at the age of thirty-nine. What happened?

To appreciate the news, we must get into the backstory. At the close of the seventh century BC, the empire of Babylon was on the verge of defeating the empire of Assyria. The winner would gain control of the Tigris-Euphrates River valley, and the deciding battle of this war was set to occur at Carchemish, 350 miles northeast of Megiddo.

But as this battle was taking shape, Egypt inserted itself into the story in order to prop up the flagging Assyrians. This meant marching the Egyptian army through Israel on the way to Carchemish. And that's where Josiah enters the story. He was determined to impede the Egyptian advance, even though his army was smaller, less adequately trained, and not as well equipped.

And that's how Megiddo comes into the story. Josiah chose to impede Egypt's advance using the Megiddo Pass, which is where the International Highway traversed Mount Carmel. The pass, southwest of the town of Megiddo, was narrow and allowed only a handful of soldiers to advance at a time. It was the one place along Egypt's route where a smaller army would have any chance against a larger force.

Josiah was killed in battle near Megiddo after he presumed that his plan was the same as the Lord's. It wasn't!

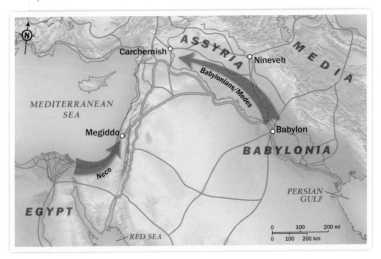

But there was also a theological reason for Josiah's choice of the plain of Megiddo. Here the Lord had repeatedly given Israel unexpected victories despite being overmatched. For example, here Gideon's 300 soldiers won a victory over thousands of desert invaders (Judg. 7). Here Deborah and Barak overcame the army of Hazor that boasted 900 iron-clad chariots (Judg. 4–5). And here Elijah overcame the 450 prophets of Baal (1 Kings 18). King Josiah presumed the plain of Megiddo would witness yet another unexpected victory—his own.

But that isn't what happened. The Egyptian army bowled over Israel and continued to Carchemish. And when the dust settled, King Josiah was dead. To appreciate this surprising turn of events, consider what's missing from the story. At no time do we hear that Josiah took this matter before the Lord. If he had consulted the Lord, he'd have learned that Egypt's plan, no matter how distasteful, was from the Lord.

And therein lies the word of caution to us. No matter how logistically possible and spiritually advantageous we may find a task, it's imperative that we consult the Lord. Otherwise, like Josiah, we might find ourselves on the wrong side of divine ambitions.

🐟 Has there been a time you proceeded with an important decision in life without consulting the Lord? What led you into that trap?

🐟 How can you use this story to speak with others about significant decisions they are making?

Father, I always want my life choices to parallel your desires. When everything seems to be going right, I'm tempted to pass over prayer. Particularly at those times, let me pause and consult you to ensure that my plan aligns with yours.

Mount Arbel

Mount Arbel National Park

Therefore go and make disciples of all nations.
Matthew 28:19

There are many stunning views in Israel, but none is more spectacular than the one offered from the summit of Mount Arbel. Here, where words fail to adequately capture the vista, Jesus spoke the resounding words that close the book of Matthew. We know them as the Great Commission.

Most visitors to Israel will encounter Mount Arbel from the shoreline of the Sea of Galilee. Although the lake is ringed by rising terrain, Mount Arbel stands out due to its dramatic profile. Its near-vertical northeastern face plunges into the valley below. But it's the view from the summit that takes our breath away. The sheer 1,280-foot drop to the lake puts the entire lake basin in view. And when you lift your eyes to the horizon, there's nothing to impede the visual spectacle

This stunning view from the summit of Mount Arbel complemented the words of the Great Commission.

until reaching distant mountains—the dome of Mount Tabor twelve miles to the southwest, the mountains of Upper Galilee fourteen miles to the northwest, and the snow-covered summit of Mount Hermon forty miles to the northeast. The panorama is postcard perfect.

This place, which is glorious on its own, becomes even more exceptional when we listen to Jesus speak the words of the Great Commission from its summit. After his resurrection and before his ascension, Jesus told his disciples to leave Jerusalem and meet him in Galilee. Matthew repeats the instructions three times (Matt. 26:32; 28:7, 10), adding the rather vague statement that the disciples went to "the mountain where Jesus had told them to go" (28:16). How do we deduce Mount Arbel from that?

To start with, it's in Galilee. It's distinguished from other mountains. It's familiar to the disciples, likely the same place where Jesus delivered the extensive discourse we call the Sermon on the Mount (Matt. 5–7), and given Jesus's penchant for linking lesson and landscape, the scene supports his message.

The Great Commission called for changes. Prior to this, Jesus had severely restricted what the disciples could tell others (Matt. 12:16; 16:20). Now he tells them to teach "everything I have commanded you" (28:20). And although Jesus once limited the scope of their ministry to "the lost sheep of Israel" (10:5–6), he now calls for a mission that will stretch to "all nations" (28:19).

In this place where Jesus had taught them his kingdom values and with a view stretching to the farthest horizon, we find the perfect backdrop for the words that define the disciples' mission and our own.

When we're tempted to think too small, to reduce the mission of the church to something more manageable, Mount Arbel resets our vision. We dare not limit the scope of the call. The gospel needs spreading, and the far horizon is calling.

🌼 Why are we so prone to artificially limit the scope of the church's mission?

🌼 How has the setting of Mount Arbel changed the way you hear the words of Jesus in the Great Commission?

Lord Jesus, you won salvation for the world. And now you ask me to lift my eyes to the far horizon and deliver the gospel to all nations. Please give me the courage, energy, and means to honor the assignment.

Mount Carmel
Monastery of Mukhraqa

———— **1 KINGS 18:1, 18–46** ————

So Ahab sent word throughout all Israel and assembled the prophets on Mount Carmel. Elijah went before the people and said, "How long will you waver between two opinions? If the LORD is God, follow him; but if Baal is God, follow him."

1 Kings 18:20–21

A handful of Carmelite monks still live in the isolated Mukhraqa monastery on Mount Carmel. They trace their heritage to Crusader knights who believed this to be *al-mukhraqa* ("the place of the sacrifice"), the setting for the contest described in 1 Kings 18.

The contest between Elijah and the prophets of Baal revolved around the question of divine authenticity. The Lord revealed himself to ancient Israel as the only authentic deity. The pagan nations had a different perspective. Immersed in a natural world they couldn't explain, they ascribed inexplicable, natural phenomena to the work of unseen deities. This included Baal, the deity thought to control dew and rainfall.

Unfortunately, ancient Israel adopted the thinking of their pagan neighbors. We see it particularly in the experience of King Ahab, who elevated Baal to the position of Israel's national deity (1 Kings 16:31–32), fueling popular support for him and causing many in Israel to waver on whether Baal or the Lord was the real deal.

All this led to the contest described in 1 Kings 18, in which each deity was given the chance to prove their authenticity. Both claimed to control the same atmospheric phenomena. Baal was often pictured riding on the top of a cumulonimbus cloud and brandishing a lightning bolt. The Lord was described with the same imagery (Exod. 19:16; Ps. 18:12, 14). Which of the two would show their legitimacy by slinging fire to earth?

Let's add location to the story. Elijah chose Mount Carmel for the contest. This arching ridge stretches for thirty miles before dipping its toes in the Mediterranean Sea. It's perfectly positioned to intercept the winter rainstorms that come off the sea, receiving far more precipitation

This relief carving, which dates from the fifteenth to thirteenth centuries BC, depicts the storm deity Baal, who failed to perform as his followers expected on Mount Carmel.

than other nearby locations. As a result, this vegetation-filled mountain became intimately connected with the worship of rain-providing, thunderbolt-wielding Baal. It was where Baal's devotees expected him to perform at his peak.

That only served to make Baal's failure more egregious. Although Baal's priests poked and prodded him all day, there was no response from this popular god. But when Elijah prayed, the Lord hurled fire from the sky, igniting the sacrifice and evaporating the altar, and then sent a series of heavy rainstorms that broke the three-year drought.

The Lord is the real deal, the only true God. But we live in a world where that isn't a popular perspective. And like Israel, our confidence in God's distinction can erode, leaving us to "waver between two opinions." This Mount Carmel story calls for us to assert afresh, "The LORD—he is God!" (1 Kings 18:39).

🌿 How has popular opinion misshaped our understanding of who God is?

🌿 How can the church best restore a correct understanding of who God is in a world that misunderstands his identity?

Father, I'm susceptible to popular opinion that misrepresents who you are. Please take me back into your Word regularly so that I can sustain a correct understanding of who you are and all you can do.

Mount Hermon

Har Bental

──── MATTHEW 17:1–9 ────

> This is my Son, whom I love; with him I am well pleased. Listen to him!
>
> Matthew 17:5

Drive north on any road in Israel and Mount Hermon will slowly rise until it fills the windshield. But for the best view of this limestone behemoth, I like Har Bental in the Golan Heights. From here I can consider the role the mountain played in Jesus's transfiguration.

When telling that story, Matthew doesn't use the proper name for this rising terrain but calls it a "high mountain" (Matt. 17:1). If you know the landscape, that's enough. Mount Hermon is 9,232 feet in elevation, 2.3 times higher than its nearest competitor. It's impossible to miss this sprawling, snow-laden ridge that dominates Israel's northern horizon.

Why does Jesus take the disciples onto its flanks in our story? First, it was nearby. Jesus and the disciples were in the region of Caesarea Philippi near the base of Mount Hermon (Matt. 16:13).

Jesus chose Mount Hermon as the "high mountain" for his transfiguration.

But second, and more importantly, Jesus used Mount Hermon as his Father had used Mount Sinai at the time of Moses. The high mountain setting signals that the Lord is about to say something particularly important. In the case of Mount Sinai, it was the giving of the law. In the case of Mount Hermon, it was marking the divinity of Jesus through the transfiguration.

Peter got the connection between these two moments in history. In the book of 2 Peter, he describes Mount Hermon with the same language used to describe both Mount Sinai and Mount Zion, calling it "the sacred mountain" (1:18; compare Exod. 19:23; Ps. 2:6; Jer. 31:23).

Now that the story's setting has our attention, it's time to consider the purpose of the transfiguration itself. It addressed a support problem. Jesus had recently revealed unthinkable details about his imminent trip to Jerusalem. There he would suffer and die before rising from the dead (Matt. 16:21). The disciples found it easy to nod in approval when Jesus spoke of easy things, but this wasn't one of those moments. The words were barely out of Jesus's mouth when Peter rebuked him: "'Never, Lord!' he said. 'This shall never happen to you!'" (16:22).

What happened next dismantled those objections. On the mountain, Jesus's appearance changed to reveal his divine glory. Moses and Elijah appeared and began talking approvingly about the trip to Jerusalem (Matt. 17:3; Luke 9:31). And then the ultimate affirmation came directly from the Father: "This is my Son, whom I love; with him I am well pleased. Listen to him!" (Matt. 17:5).

Many of the things Jesus says to us are pleasant and easy to hear. But when he speaks about things that are less pleasant and harder to accept, he calls us back to the high ground of Mount Hermon to solidify our trust. Jesus is God's Son, the one worthy of our attention whether he's speaking of easy things or hard.

Make a list of the hard things Jesus has asked you to believe. Which of them is the most difficult for you?

What role does Jesus's transfiguration play in how you listen to Jesus?

Lord Jesus, I confess that there are times when I resist the things you say. Please break down my stubborn defiance. Use your transfiguration to remind me that there's nothing ordinary about you, and lead me to accept all you teach without objection.

Mount of Olives

Church of All Nations

MATTHEW 26:36–46

Then he returned to the disciples and said to them, "Are you still sleeping and resting? Look, the hour has come, and the Son of Man is delivered into the hands of sinners."

Matthew 26:45

The Church of All Nations protects an unassuming piece of bedrock regarded for centuries as the place of Jesus's Gethsemane prayer. As we walk past the olive trees and enter the quiet, darkened sanctuary, we contemplate Jesus's struggle here.

The Gospel writers signal that this experience of Jesus is like no other. The language they use to describe his mental and emotional state is used only here and only of Jesus: "sorrowful and troubled" (Matt. 26:37), "distressed" (Mark 14:33), and "in anguish" (Luke 22:44). Matthew speaks of Jesus's posture. He doesn't kneel before a boulder with hands clasped, as so often pictured, but sprawls facedown on the ground (Matt. 26:39).

And then there are Jesus's words. We have never heard him speak like this. He knows he's going to die and face the punishment for all sins of all time, and he's pleading with the Father for an alternative (Matt. 26:38–39).

All those details are unique and powerful, but I find the most compelling words of this story to be these: "he returned" (Matt. 26:45). Jesus was on the west side of the Mount of Olives, a two-mile ridge that lies between the city of Jerusalem and the Judean wilderness. The wilderness is a dry, tortured landscape so hostile to human survival that it remains empty to this day. That makes it the perfect place for a person to hide from anyone intending to harm them. That was how David used it when his son Absalom marched an army against Jerusalem to wrest the throne from him. Not wishing the city to be harmed, David fled east through the

The Church of All Nations marks the traditional location of Jesus's struggle in prayer on the Mount of Olives.

Kidron Valley, right past the garden of Gethsemane, over the ridge of the Mount of Olives, and into the Judean wilderness (2 Sam. 15:23–30). It's as if David had blazed a trail for Jesus to follow. By walking east for a little more than half an hour, Jesus could have been free from all the harm to come.

Only when we appreciate the place of Jesus's struggle will we find the power in the phrase "he returned." Jesus faced a choice. And it was real. As I watch and listen to this story unfold, I feel my eternal destiny hanging in the balance. If Jesus had done what was best for him, he would have walked east and disappeared into the wilderness. But instead, he did what was best for you and me. He returned. His voice, filled with decisive determination, says, "Rise! Let us go! Here comes my betrayer!" (Matt. 26:46).

🔖 Describe a time when you were in a place that influenced an important decision.

🔖 How does the geography of this familiar story from the Gospels change the way you read and apply it to your life?

Lord Jesus, I feel renewed appreciation for how difficult the Gethsemane moment was for you. And I'm filled with gratitude for the decision you made there. You didn't do what was best for you but what was best for me. Let me now live my life in grateful thanks.

Mount of Olives

Church of the Pater Noster

LUKE 11:1–4

One day Jesus was praying in a certain place. When he finished, one of his disciples said to him, "Lord, teach us to pray."

Luke 11:1

The history of the Church of the Pater Noster compound is a bit complicated. The first Christian church on this site was built in the fourth century AD when Helena, mother of the Roman emperor Constantine, commissioned a basilica to commemorate Jesus's ascension from the Mount of Olives. The earliest visitors called it Eleona Church (Greek for "olive grove").

By the twelfth century, the focus had shifted to a nearby cave. The Crusaders believed this was the "certain place" (Luke 11:1) where Jesus reviewed the lesson on prayer that he had first given in Galilee (Matt. 6:9–13). This leads to the more popular name for the location today: the Church of the Pater Noster (Latin for "Our Father").

This ceramic plaque at the Church of the Pater Noster presents the Lord's Prayer in Latin and invites us to think about how we pray.

For me, the power of the place is in the cloister. The cloister consists of several covered hallways lined with near-identical ceramic plaques, each emblazoned with the words of the Lord's Prayer in a different language. As I walk the hallways, no matter where I look, I'm surrounded by the prayer Jesus himself taught us to pray.

The experience does two things for me. First, every step I take brings me before another plaque with the words "Our Father." This refrain reminds me that the Lord is the head of the human household. In the first century, the head of the extended family household was vitally interested in the well-being of its members and fully capable of giving them the things they needed. It doesn't matter what place I call home, my family situation, or what language I speak—God is my Father. He is the one to whom I pray. Jesus's Father is also my Father (Rom. 8:14–17; Gal. 4:4–7).

Second, this walk through the cloister reminds me to balance my prayer life. I often ask for things I need: food, forgiveness, spiritual strength. All are appropriate and in the Lord's Prayer model. But before I ask for those things, this paradigm for Christian prayer urges me to think of what the Lord wants: his name kept holy and his kingdom advanced.

Here I stop, close my eyes, and listen. Other members of the Lord's family, each in their own language, are praying the words that teach us how to pray. I cannot help but join in.

❧ How does the image of God as our Father shape your prayer life?

❧ Where are you most challenged in balancing your prayer requests?

Lord Jesus, today I join with the disciples in asking you to teach me to pray well. I confess that I have been less thoughtful about who I'm praying to and that my prayer life has become imbalanced. Please use this moment at the Church of the Pater Noster to improve how I pray.

Mount of Olives

Dominus Flevit Church

As he approached Jerusalem and saw the city, he wept over it and said, "If you, even you, had only known on this day what would bring you peace—but now it is hidden from your eyes."

Luke 19:41–42

The teardrop shape of the Dominus Flevit Church symbolizes the deep grief that seized Jesus as he entered Jerusalem. Even as the Palm Sunday crowds celebrated his arrival, Jesus wept.

We won't fully appreciate this Jerusalem arrival unless we see how intentionally unique it was. Jesus had entered Jerusalem many times in his life, but never like this.

First, Jesus chose to enter the Holy City from the east instead of taking his more typical northern route. The Gospel writers emphasize the direction of his arrival with place names like Jericho, Bethany, Bethphage, and Mount of Olives. This means Jesus was approaching Jerusalem from the direction the Old Testament prophets associated with the

This modern view of Jerusalem through the window of the Dominus Flevit Church commemorates the view Jesus had of the Holy City that brought him to tears.

Messiah (Isa. 40:3; Zech. 14:4), "the sun of righteousness [that] will rise with healing in its rays" (Mal. 4:2).

Second, Jesus rode a donkey into Jerusalem. Not only is this the first time we read of Jesus riding an animal, but he was also riding into the Holy City just as the prophet Zechariah anticipated the Messiah would (Zech. 9:9).

There's one more thing: the relationship between Jesus's arrival route and the Gihon Spring. It's unreported in the Gospels but lives on the landscape. Jesus was riding down the west side of the Mount of Olives toward this spring. The prophets don't speak to this, but history does. In the tenth century BC, King David ordered that his son Solomon be put on David's mule and escorted to the Gihon Spring. There Solomon was anointed as Israel's next king (1 Kings 1:32–35).

The Palm Sunday crowds saw history repeating itself. Jesus was riding a donkey in the direction of the Gihon Spring for an apparent coronation like that of Solomon (Matt. 21:9; Mark 11:10; Luke 19:38). They exploded in celebration.

So what made Jesus weep? Jesus strategically entered Jerusalem to announce himself as the Messiah, the King of Israel. But many saw him simply as a king who would liberate them from the Roman occupation. Disappointment would soon replace their celebration, because this King humbled himself to the point of dying on a cross to bring peace between God and sinners. By the following Sunday, Rome would still rule, but Satan would be dethroned.

Jesus wept because Jerusalem missed it. Do we? Whom do we see or want to see in Jesus? Do we value him for who he is? Is Jesus weeping over our response?

🐾 How have you seen the core mission of Jesus misrepresented today?

🐾 How can you use the Palm Sunday arrival of Jesus to keep your eyes fixed on the purpose for which he came?

Lord Jesus, there's the risk I'll miss the very reason you came into the world and cause you to weep again. Please anchor my perception of you in the reality of your mission. Let me honor you today as the King who came to save me from my sin.

Mount Tabor

Jezreel Valley

Then Deborah said to Barak, "Go! This is the day the LORD has given Sisera into your hands. Has not the LORD gone ahead of you?"

Judges 4:14

I enjoy driving through the Jezreel Valley beneath the dome of Mount Tabor. This rural, serene landscape lends a sense of calm to the busiest of days. But this setting was anything but calm at the time of Deborah and Barak. Imagine the plain filled with invaders from the Canaanite city-state of Hazor. Imagine row after row of iron-clad chariots—nine hundred of them—technology for which ancient Israel had no answer. This disturbing scene was fostered by a larger problem in Israel: they had lost faith in the Lord and contaminated the promised land with their worship of other gods. To call them to account, the Lord had allowed Hazor to dominate Israel for twenty years.

Mount Tabor plays a key role in the faith lesson taught through the story of Deborah and Barak.

The prophet Deborah summoned Israel's general, Barak, to initiate a solution. She instructed him to muster the tribal militias on Mount Tabor. If there was to be a fight, this is where the Israelite infantry wanted to have it. The wooded slopes of Mount Tabor rise abruptly from the valley floor, precluding the use of chariots. Barak's plan was to lure the enemy into abandoning their chariots on the plain for a fight on the mountain slopes. Here Israel's infantry was better matched against the invaders, plus they had already gained the high ground. The invaders would have to fight uphill. All in all, this was the best Israel could've hoped for.

The Lord was about to ask something unexpected.

Deborah called for Barak to leave the high ground and charge the chariots on the plain. This made no sense. Pitting foot soldiers against a chariot corps was a suicide mission. But more than that, it was a call to trust the Lord.

At this critical moment, Israel stepped out in faith and the Lord stepped up in power. The narrative account simply states that the Canaanites were routed (Judg. 4:15), but Deborah's poetic account in chapter 5 describes how God did it. It's true that chariots on dry ground would have the advantage over infantry troops, but the ground didn't stay dry for long. The Lord sent an off-season thunderstorm so violent and intense that it swamped the valley floor (5:4, 21). The chariots bogged down in the mud, becoming easy targets for Israel's infantry. Faith carried Israel from the safe slopes of Tabor to the threatening plain where the Lord gave them victory.

Today is no different. Common sense leads us to make safe choices. But be ready. The Lord may call you to do something that defies common sense. Know that when he does, the Lord has "gone ahead of you" (Judg. 4:14).

❧ What is your Mount Tabor, the safe zone from which you prefer to operate?

❧ When has the Lord called you to abandon the mountain for the plain, summoning you to trust beyond the bounds of common sense?

Heavenly Father, when I'm confronted by circumstances that loom like nine hundred iron-clad chariots, strengthen my faith. Give me the trust I need to do the unthinkable, knowing that you can do the impossible.

Nablus

Church of Jacob's Well

So he came to a town in Samaria called Sychar, near the plot
of ground Jacob had given to his son Joseph. Jacob's well was
there.

John 4:5–6

I can hear Jacob's Well as vividly as I see it. The old
limestone well cap sports a rusty winch with a gnarled
rope wrapped around it that visitors use to draw water
from this ancient well. Every time the leaky bucket is lowered or raised, the pulley objects with groans and squeaks.
But it's a different sound that brings us here—the sound of
Jesus's voice.

You'd never guess that a beautiful church resides behind
the spartan, steel doors that guard the entry to the compound. Ringing the bell summons the Greek Orthodox
priest, who gives the warm welcome this place has offered
to Jesus's followers since the fourth century AD when the

Jacob's Well in Samaria marks the spot that waited for the coming of the Messiah longer than any other location in the promised land.

first church was built around the well. Like other visitors through the years, we've come to listen in on a long conversation between Jesus and the Samaritan woman who called nearby Sychar home.

This New Testament story from John 4 repeatedly draws us to the heart of the Old Testament, as Jacob is mentioned three times (vv. 5, 6, 12). Upon his return from Paddan Aram, Jacob purchased this tract of land and dug the very well we are visiting (Gen. 33:18–20).

The woman in John 4 mentions her "ancestors" who worshiped on this mountain (v. 20). Given that the holy book of the Samaritans was limited to the Torah (Pentateuch), she was speaking about Abraham and Sarah's family, who didn't know the place as Sychar (its New Testament name) but as Shechem. The Lord had a mission for this family, linking the Savior from sin both to them and to the promised land (Gen. 12:1–7). When Abraham and Sarah arrived at the mountain pass that hosts Shechem/Sychar, the Lord confirmed they had reached their destination. Abraham immediately built an altar here and worshiped in the promised land for the first time. For the next seven hundred years, Shechem, not Shiloh or Jerusalem, was the geographic center of Israel's worship life.

And that's why Jesus had to come to Sychar. He wasn't initiating a religious story but was continuing an Old Testament story that began at the time of Abraham and Sarah. And what better place to make that point than the place within the promised land that had waited longest for his arrival?

The conversation between Jesus and the Samaritan woman changed topics several times, but they eventually came around to the topic of worship. Here, at Israel's very first sacred worship site, Jesus did something he would do only one other time in one other location: he verbally declared that he was the Messiah. "I, the one speaking to you—I am he" (John 4:26).

This wasn't just a random place Jesus went but a place he "had to go" (John 4:4). Here Jesus uses geography to build a visual, tangible bridge between himself and the Old Testament prophecies about the Messiah. When we listen for the geography, we will hear it as surely as we hear the creak of the old winch of Jacob's Well.

🪶 The Old Testament gets less attention from Christian readers than the New. Why do you think that is the case?

🪶 Why is it important for us to see that the mission of Jesus has deep roots in the Old Testament?

Lord Jesus, forgive me for trying to understand who you are and why you came without anchoring your story in the Old Testament. Make me a better student of the past so that I can better understand you and your connection to my present.

Nazareth

Church of the Annunciation

"I am the Lord's servant," Mary answered. "May your word to me be fulfilled." Then the angel left her.

Luke 1:38

The Church (or Basilica) of the Annunciation marks the location long associated with Gabriel's visit to Mary. It's a place for us to consider just how challenging her assignment was and how faithfully she responded.

Let's start by fixing the picture of Nazareth. The modern city creeps up and over ridges that once contained it, allowing its current population to explode to more than a hundred thousand people. First-century Nazareth was nestled into the valley floor, enclosed by ridges, with room for just a few dozen households and no more than four hundred residents. The world could not see in, and that's just the way the people of Nazareth liked it.

Citizens of Nazareth were subsistence farmers who remained isolated from world markets and from the pagan ideology that had gripped much of the promised land. Obedience to Torah took pride of place here. In Nazareth, you arranged your daughter's marriage before she was thirteen and expected her to become pregnant only after the marriage ceremony.

To appreciate Mary's assignment, we need to take a careful look at the exchanges during Gabriel's visit. Let's start with the fact that this young teen was visited by an angel. Not sure how I might have done with that! Gabriel's words cut deeply into the heart of Old Testament promises about a Savior from sin who would be descended from King David. Building to a crescendo, he revealed that Mary's son would be *the* descendant of David who would rule an eternal kingdom.

The grotto of the nativity at the Church of the Annunciation in Nazareth marks the traditional spot for Gabriel's meeting with Mary.

There was a hitch, though: the conception would involve a miracle. Mary would become pregnant by the Holy Spirit before her wedding day and without Joseph's involvement. And at just the moment Mary must have been steeling herself to tell this news to Joseph, their families, and the village, Gabriel left her. We need to feel the absence. Mary went to deliver the news by herself—news that even Joseph found impossible to believe.

The stunning revelation is followed by an equally stunning response. Mary replied to everything the angel told her by essentially saying, "Okay." Given how dramatically and suddenly the news was sprung, I doubt she fully understood it all. We still don't understand it today. But she quickly calculated the social challenges and didn't beg off the assignment or ask for time to think about it.

Mary's response challenges us. We like assignments we can understand and that promise to improve the quality of our lives. But the Lord may ask us to take on a task we don't understand, don't like, or find socially unpopular. May we respond with the faith, resolve, and confidence of Mary, who said, "I am the Lord's servant" (Luke 1:38).

🐚 What most impresses you about Mary's response to the challenge Gabriel's message put into her life?

🐚 When has the Lord asked you to do something you didn't fully understand or desire? How did you respond?

Lord, thank you for Mary. Not only did she give birth to Jesus, my Savior, but she also shows me how to respond to difficult assignments. Help me respond with the same faith, courage, and confidence she displayed.

Nazareth
Church of Saint Joseph

MATTHEW 1:18–25

The Lord appeared to him in a dream and said, "Joseph son of David, do not be afraid to take Mary home as your wife."

Matthew 1:20

Nazareth's Church of Saint Joseph gets far less attention than the neighboring Church of the Annunciation. The latter's modern design, soaring cupola, and connection to the Virgin Mary guarantee that the church named in Joseph's honor, like Joseph himself, fades into the background. And therein lies a lesson.

The Church of Saint Joseph was built in 1914 over the footprint of a twelfth-century Crusader church connected to the traditional home and workshop of Joseph's family. By trade, Joseph was a builder, a man comfortable working with his hands. He was the village handyman who people turned to when they needed something built or made, whether that

This art installation at the Church of Saint Joseph in Nazareth recalls the important role Joseph played in Jesus's life.

was a stone foundation for a house or a wooden plow for the field.

This humble man was caught up in a scandal. The story spread like wildfire, as scandalous stories do in towns with only a dozen or so households. Joseph's and Mary's parents had arranged their marriage. The financial details were in place, the wedding agreement had been signed, and everyone was waiting for the wedding day. Then the news of Mary's pregnancy dropped, and all eyes turned to the kindly Joseph. What was he going to do?

Given his social context, Joseph saw two options—not good and bad but bad and worse. He could publicly divorce Mary. This meant denouncing her in a public meeting before the village elders, exonerating himself, and leaving Mary to absorb the village's response.

The other alternative was a private or quiet divorce. In this case, there would be no public airing of grievances. Two or three witnesses would give testimony, and the marriage contract would be annulled. Joseph had decided on this second option, leaving questions about his role in the pregnancy and deflecting some of the social stigma onto himself.

That's when the Lord sent an angel with a third option: "Do not be afraid to take Mary home as your wife" (Matt. 1:20). This would permanently connect Joseph to the scandal, but it was the only choice that enabled him to play his role. He wasn't Jesus's biological father, but he would do what all Jewish fathers and stepfathers did: give his son the legal connection to Israel's family tree. We hear subtle reference to this role in the first words the angel spoke to him: "Joseph son of David." Being descended from King David was a prerequisite for the Messiah, and it was Joseph, not Mary, who linked Jesus to David's family tree.

Most of us are people like Joseph, quietly making our contribution to the kingdom. Take a moment at the Church of Saint Joseph to ponder your connection to this wonderful man and to feel the appreciation of a grateful church.

🌿 What about Joseph's work do you find most compelling in this story?

🌿 How do you see Joseph's character as a model for your service?

Heavenly Father, excite me for the role you have for me to play in the church, no matter how inconsequential it may seem. Let me be like Joseph, out of the public spotlight but deeply set in your heart.

Nazareth

Mount Precipice

They got up, drove him out of the town, and took him to the brow of the hill on which the town was built, in order to throw him off the cliff.

Luke 4:29

Mount Precipice is part of the near-vertical Nazareth Ridge that lies just south of the city of Nazareth. In Jesus's day, it offered a look into two different worlds. To the south was the Jezreel Valley, an international transportation corridor filled with gentiles. To the north was the isolated hamlet of Nazareth. Trouble came to this ridge when Jesus tried to bridge these two worlds.

The archaeology and geography of Nazareth paint a picture of life in Jesus's hometown. Its residents chose to isolate themselves from the gentile world in a bid to maintain their connection to the faith of their forebearers. They expected their children to do the same.

The people of Jesus's hometown tried to execute him using this precipitous ridge called Mount Precipice. Their anger was triggered by Jesus's vision of a kingdom more inclusive than the one they expected.

As long as Jesus fit that picture, Nazareth loved him. When invited to speak in the synagogue, Jesus stood to read the Scripture lesson for the day in Hebrew. Then he sat down to teach on the passage in Aramaic. After reading an Old Testament prophecy related to the coming Messiah, he declared, "Today this scripture is fulfilled in your hearing" (Luke 4:21). And the people loved it and loved him.

Then things took a dark turn. Some noticed that Jesus had left out a line from the Isaiah reading—the one that spoke about "the day of vengeance of our God" (Isa. 61:2), retribution directed at gentiles. Raised eyebrows soon turned to rage.

Jesus continued by holding up as examples two noble gentiles who had accepted the Lord when others in Israel had rejected him: the widow of Zarephath in Sidon from the time of Elijah, and Naaman the Syrian from the time of Elisha. Outrageous! Hating the message, the people of Nazareth sought to kill the messenger. They whisked Jesus to the brow of the hill called Mount Precipice, intending to throw him off so that he could be with the gentile world for which he had expressed such affection.

Jesus loved Nazareth. As someone who spent most of his life among these people, Jesus understood how the current Roman occupation of the promised land that came on the heels of so many other international occupations fueled a distaste for gentiles that bordered on hate. But hometown or not, this had to change.

And it must change in us too. We also are prone to think that the church should look like the person we see in the mirror. May our church be as diverse as the world that Jesus came to save.

🌱 Does your church look like the community around it? If so, why? If not, why not?

🌱 How can you help your church be as diverse as the world for which Jesus died?

Lord Jesus, forgive me for ignoring those who *are unlike me. Let your church be as diverse as the world you came to redeem.*

Qumran

Qumran National Park

"I baptize with water," John replied, "but among you stands one you do not know. He is the one who comes after me, the straps of whose sandals I am not worthy to untie."

John 1:26–27

The ruins at Qumran on the northwest shore of the Dead Sea offer a wonderful view of the arena in which John the Baptist ministered. And his ministry reminds us how important it is to stay in our lane.

It won't take long to walk through the archaeological site of Qumran. It's only 330 feet long by 260 feet wide. But you don't want to miss the scriptorium. Long, plastered writing benches once filled this room. Dozens of people sat here, pen in hand, ready to copy down the words read from the podium at the front of the room. This was as close as you could get to having a photocopier in the ancient world. Some of this copied literature was stored in the local cave systems and became known as the Dead Sea Scrolls.

There are quite a few similarities between John the Baptist and the Essene community that copied these documents. They were active at the same time in the same general location. They both made daily ceremonial use of water. They both had left Jerusalem for the wilderness to await the coming of change, seeing themselves in the language of Isaiah 40:1–3. It is no wonder that many scholars presume John was part of this community at Qumran. That conversation continues.

Let's sidestep that discussion for the moment and move to the view northeast from Qumran, a view toward the final miles of the Jordan River before it enters the Dead Sea. This is where we find "Bethany on the other side of the Jordan" (John 1:28), a place John frequented. The Lord called this man to prepare the hearts and minds of his listeners to meet God face-to-face.

According to Isaiah 40, the Messiah would appear in the wilderness where John was preaching and baptizing. Crowds flocked to him, and many people wanted to

Inkwells like these were used by the community at Qumran when copying the ancient documents known as the Dead Sea Scrolls.

assign him a title and role other than the one God gave him. It would've been easy for John to revel in this popularity and get out of his lane. Yet John resisted that temptation and relentlessly directed attention away from himself to Jesus: "I am not the Messiah" (John 1:20). "He is the one who comes after me, the straps of whose sandals I am not worthy to untie" (1:27). "The reason I came baptizing with water was that he might be revealed to Israel" (1:31).

The Lord has called us to play a role in the kingdom. We also may be tempted to take on roles that have been given to others. The story of John unfolding in the view from Qumran reminds us to stay in our lane.

⚜ What role(s) has the Lord asked you to play in his kingdom?

⚜ What makes it difficult for you to stay in that ministry lane?

Lord Jesus, you are the Lord of the church. Help me define and accept the role you have given me to play in it. Defeat the jealousy or dissatisfaction that tempts me to get out of my ministry lane.

Samaria/Sebaste

Tel Shomron

---

1 KINGS 16:23–34; ACTS 8:4–17

> When the crowds heard Philip and saw the signs he performed, they all paid close attention to what he said.
>
> Acts 8:6

Samaria/Sebaste resides on a low, rounded hill that rises above a rich agricultural basin. It looks idyllic. But it's a place with a dark backstory, making it the perfect test case for this question: Can a place become too sin-ruined to save?

The city's story begins with King Omri in the ninth century BC. He founded this municipality as the capital of Israel's northern kingdom shortly before negotiating a trade deal with Phoenicia. Omri had trade goods to move to market. Phoenicia had a distribution system that included a fleet of ships and harbors throughout the Mediterranean world. It was a perfect commercial match. The deal was sealed by the

This staircase led up to the temple of Augustus at Sebaste. Was this a place too sin-ruined to save?

marriage of a Phoenician princess to a prince of Israel—the infamous era of Ahab and Jezebel had begun.

When Jezebel left Phoenicia, she brought along her love for Baal and convinced Ahab that his economic success was linked to this deity. They built a temple to Baal in Samaria, effectively making Baal, rather than the Lord, their chief national deity. This guaranteed Ahab would receive a negative evaluation and that Samaria would be linked to his legacy (1 Kings 16:31–32).

Eight hundred years later, the city's reputation hadn't improved. Herod the Great rebuilt Samaria, and on the same high point of the city where the temple of Baal had likely stood, he built a temple to the Roman emperor Caesar Augustus. Today a ninety-foot-wide staircase associated with this temple still marks the spot. Herod renamed the city Sebaste, the Greek equivalent of Augustus, assuring that its legacy as a pagan, sin-ruined city continued.

Then along came the evangelist Philip. Persecution had driven him from Jerusalem, and when he arrived in the city of Samaria/Sebaste, he seemed unfazed by its ruinous reputation. He spoke about Jesus, and the people listened and believed. If Philip was surprised by all this, the believers in Jerusalem were shocked: "When the apostles in Jerusalem heard that Samaria had accepted the word of God, they sent Peter and John to Samaria" (Acts 8:14).

But when the two apostles arrived, they found the report to be true. They laid their hands on these new believers and prayed for them. When they did, the Spirit came on them just as he had come on the believers in Jerusalem at Pentecost. The Holy City and Samaria now shared a similar story to signal that no place, not even one as damaged as Samaria, is too sin-ruined to save.

And that offers a powerful corrective to our mindset today. It's easy to fall into the trap of thinking that certain people or places are so far gone that the gospel couldn't benefit them. Samaria/Sebaste proves that no place or person can out-sin the reach of God's forgiveness.

❧ What group, place, or person might be the equivalent of Samaria/Sebaste in our minds today?

❧ How does this story from Samaria/Sebaste bring hope to you today?

Holy Spirit, you clearly are capable of more than I sometimes imagine. Please keep me from thinking there are people or places too sin-ruined to save—including myself.

Sea of Galilee

Ginnosar Boat Museum

MATTHEW 14:22–33

Immediately Jesus reached out his hand and caught him.

Matthew 14:31

The shoreline of the Sea of Galilee is the setting for many stories from the life of Jesus. A number of these are boat stories that take place on the surface of the lake, including the one in Matthew 14, which highlights the way Jesus responds to people like you and me who often exhibit imperfect faith.

The Sea of Galilee is the freshwater inland lake that fills a low-elevation basin in northern Israel. Today tour boats and kiteboards dot its surface. But in Jesus's day, the lake pulsed with a thriving fishing industry and was studded with no less than twenty-seven harbors. Four of Jesus's disciples were connected to the fishing trade, including Peter.

In 1986, when drought lowered the lake's level, two brothers discovered an ancient fishing boat that has been carbon dated to the time of Jesus. Today the lakeside Yigal Allon Museum at Ginnosar preserves the story of its discovery, recovery, and restoration and allows us to actually examine the hull. The boat is twenty-seven feet long, just large enough to hold fishing nets and a crew of about thirteen tightly packed passengers. Its shape was defined by oak ribs, and its hull was composed of cedar planks attached to the ribs using mortise and tenon joints, pegs, and nails.

In Matthew 14, Jesus had gone up on a mountainside to pray while the disciples boarded a boat much like this one for the short trip from Bethsaida to Capernaum. Given that the wind on the lake typically died down in the evening, they expected smooth sailing and a quick ride to their destination.

They didn't get either. By morning, we see them straining to make progress against the wind and waves. Then a ghostly

The surviving hull of a fishing boat from the first century AD was discovered on the Sea of Galilee and helps us picture the kind of boat frequently mentioned in the Gospels.

figure appears walking on the lake's surface and speaks to them in a familiar voice. It's Jesus! Peter says, "If that is you, Jesus, let me walk on the water to you." Jesus invites him to come, so Peter steps over the gunnel and begins to take cautious steps in Jesus's direction. But the farther he gets from the boat, the more Peter's attention shifts to the fierce wind and roiling waves. His imperfect faith weighs him down, and as he begins to sink he cries, "Lord, save me!" (Matt. 14:30).

And this gives us a chance to see how Jesus responds to people with imperfect faith. To be sure, he criticizes Peter's doubt. But first he acts: "Immediately Jesus reached out his hand and caught him" (14:31).

Like Peter, we get distracted by the wind and waves around us. Our faith, like Peter's, is imperfect. How will Jesus respond? His hand is reaching out to us even as we struggle to reach out for him.

- What are the "winds and waves" that distract you from a laser-like focus on Jesus?

- How have you sensed Jesus reaching out to you when your faith is weak?

Lord Jesus, you know all too well that I am a person with imperfect faith. Thank you for reaching out to me even when my faith has struggled to reach out to you.

Shechem

Tel Balata

GENESIS 12:1–7

> The LORD appeared to Abram and said, "To your offspring I will give this land." So he built an altar there to the LORD, who had appeared to him.
>
> Genesis 12:7

A lthough this West Bank site is rarely visited, Shechem is one of the most important places in the Holy Land. It's the first place where we hear the Lord speaking about the promise of salvation to someone who was literally standing in the Holy Land.

Shechem is located in a pass between Mount Ebal and Mount Gerizim, a place second to none in livability. It is blessed with rich agricultural land and springs that flow from Mount Ebal. Both contribute to a surplus of food that can be easily transported to markets via the road systems that converge at this topographic roundabout. It's no wonder this place enjoys a long history.

The mountain pass between Mount Ebal and Mount Gerizim was where Abraham and Sarah learned they had arrived in the promised land.

The impressive remains at Tel Balata date to more than three hundred years after Abraham and Sarah, but they mark the spot for the story told in Genesis 12. This story doesn't begin here but in Harran, nearly four hundred miles northeast of Shechem, where the Lord called Abraham and Sarah to leave their homeland and travel to a land he would show them. God gave them three stunning promises. First, they would have a family that would become a great nation. Second, one of their descendants would restore the blessing of a right relationship with God that had been lost in Eden. And third, the first two promises would be linked to a new homeland.

After weeks of travel, Abraham and Sarah arrived at Shechem, where the Lord signaled the end of their journey with these words: "To your offspring I will give this land"

(Gen. 12:7). These three promises form a triangle: Abraham and Sarah's family would become a great nation. That nation would own this land, the land of Canaan. And from that family on this land, the Messiah (Jesus) would restore peace between God and mortals.

Abraham responded by building a memorial altar at Shechem, and the Old Testament authors and poets bring us back to this place again and again. In time, Israel would establish sanctuaries at Shiloh and Jerusalem. But for seven hundred years, Shechem was THE place of worship in the promised land.

Shechem and the triangle of promises launched here shape the way the Lord intends for us to read the Old Testament. To be sure, there are a lot of laws in these books. But there's also a lot of gospel (Gal. 3:8). To see it, we need to think the way the biblical authors and poets did. Any time they mention Abraham's family, the promised land, or the restoration of blessing through the Messiah, they are using language linked to the Lord's promise to forgive sins. Standing beside Abraham and Sarah at Shechem, we can hear the gospel as they did.

🐚 What obstacles do you face when reading the Old Testament books?

🐚 How has the story of Shechem changed where you find the gospel in the Old Testament?

Heavenly Father, you are and always have been the God of love and forgiveness. Help me to see it more clearly in the Old Testament by using the gospel triangle established at Shechem.

Shiloh

Seer's Tower

JOSHUA 18:1–10; JEREMIAH 7:3–12

Go now to the place in Shiloh where I first made a dwelling for my Name, and see what I did to it because of the wickedness of my people Israel.

Jeremiah 7:12

Start your visit to Shiloh by climbing to the top of the round Seer's Tower at the center of the site. From here you can appreciate the scope of the 7.5-acre site and take in its story that stretches across eight hundred years. During those centuries, we see Shiloh change from the honored home of the Lord to an object lesson on desertion.

The Bible's first mention of Shiloh establishes its honored status. Joshua and the Israelites had successfully defeated the largest and most capable city-states in Canaan. Now it was time to set down roots, beginning with the tabernacle, which would make its home in Shiloh for the next three hundred years. This was the place where Israel came to be in the Lord's

Shiloh

Shiloh was the place where most of Israel's tribes learned the location of their assigned land parcels, as pictured in this map.

presence and to worship him (Josh. 18:1). This was also where Joshua completed the division of the land among the tribes of Israel (18:10) so that families could establish uncontested water systems and farm undisputed land. Even more importantly, it gave each family a land parcel that reminded them of the Lord's promises to bring forgiveness to the world.

By 1094 BC, Shiloh was a smoking ruin. To be sure, Samuel made a home here serving at the tabernacle. But not even his presence could stem the corruption of the high priest Eli's two sons, Hophni and Phinehas (1 Sam. 2:12–25). They allowed Israel to transport the ark of the covenant into battle against the Philistines (1 Sam. 4). The ark was captured. And although this part of the story isn't told in Scripture, the archaeology of Shiloh exposes the destruction of the city that followed.

Shiloh receives sparing mention for the next five hundred years. But it comes to the foreground again in the powerful sermon Jeremiah preached at the temple in Jerusalem just before the Babylonians destroyed it (Jer. 7:1–20). Corruption had again entered the sanctuary, but Jeremiah's calls for repentance were met with the refrain, "This is the temple of the LORD, the temple of the LORD, the temple of the LORD!" (7:4).

The mistaken assumption was that the Lord would never allow the Holy City to be harmed. That's when Jeremiah reminded them of Shiloh: "Go now to the place in Shiloh where I first made a dwelling for my Name, and see what I did to it because of the wickedness of my people Israel" (Jer. 7:12).

This is a striking call to vigilance. The Lord's presence and blessing on a place can be withdrawn by careless, wanton apostasy. Shiloh makes the Lord's position clear: better a sanctuary in ruins than one eaten through by corruption.

☙ Where have you seen corruption damage the well-being of the church?

☙ How will the story of Shiloh change the way you think about the health of your own local church?

Dear Lord, I repent of those times when I have presumed too much. Keep me from putting my trust in a place or a building rather than in you.

Shiloh

Tabernacle Plateau

Speak, for your servant is listening.

1 Samuel 3:10

Experts do not agree on where the tabernacle stood in Shiloh for the three hundred years it spent here. Some suggest it was on the south side of the site where beautiful mosaics of Byzantine church floors remain. Others suggest it was at the top of the hill on which the city was built. But I like to think it was on the north side of Shiloh, where the slope of the hill gives way to a level platform perfectly suited for the sanctuary. It's a good place to think about the consequential difference between hearing God and listening to him.

The opening of 1 Samuel is filled with tone-deaf people—all of them encircling Hannah. This godly woman struggled with infertility in a culture that emphasized her role to bear children who would grow into workers for the extended family. Hannah's trips to Shiloh introduce us to the tone-deaf cast

The tabernacle was pitched in Shiloh for over three hundred years. This worship center was the setting for a lesson about listening to God.

around her. Her husband Elkanah's second wife relentlessly mocked and belittled her. Elkanah himself just didn't get it. "Don't I mean more to you than ten sons?" (1:8). Really!

Even the religious leaders at Shiloh were hopeless. The high priest, Eli, confused Hannah's heartfelt prayer for drunkenness. Eli's two sons, Hophni and Phinehas, were "scoundrels" who had "no regard for the LORD" (2:12). They leveraged their position as priests to take what they wanted from the sacrifices and engaged in sexual misconduct with the women who also served at the Shiloh sanctuary.

In this place where God had made himself available in a unique way, people were hearing but not listening. It's no wonder that the Lord stopped speaking (3:1).

Then along came Samuel. The Lord had answered Hannah's prayer for a son, and she kept her vow to commit

Samuel's life to the Lord's service. As a young man, Samuel was the only one at the Shiloh sanctuary who was untainted. One night as Samuel slept in the sanctuary, the Lord called him: "Samuel!" Three times Samuel thought it was Eli and ran to his side. But the fourth time, Samuel replied, "Speak, for your servant is listening" (3:10).

There it was, the thing that had been missing at Shiloh. And when Samuel listened, things began to change: "The LORD continued to appear at Shiloh, and there he revealed himself to Samuel through his word" (3:21).

Many of us spend a great deal of time with the Bible in personal study, Bible study groups, and worship at our local church. This story challenges us to consider the outcome of all that time in the Word. Am I truly listening or merely hearing when God speaks?

🦋 Where do you find yourself prone to hear without listening to the Lord?

🦋 What qualities do you see in Samuel that make him an example for us to follow?

Heavenly Father, you are always eager to speak with us. And I confess that I have heard without listening. Please forgive me and change me so that I fully absorb your words and apply them to my life.

Southern Wilderness
En Avdat National Park

But the LORD said to Moses and Aaron, "Because you did not trust in me enough to honor me as holy in the sight of the Israelites, you will not bring this community into the land I give them."

Numbers 20:12

In En Avdat National Park, the Wilderness of Zin's geology is on full display—its near-vertical limestone walls are layered with seams of flint. This geological feature plays a vital role in our understanding of Moses's dramatic disqualification. At the beginning of the story in Numbers 20, we expect him to lead Israel into the promised land. By the story's conclusion, we know he won't.

This story opens in the final days of Israel's four-decade stay in the southern wilderness. The lack of natural resources has once again contributed to the people's rebellion against the Lord's appointed leaders. "Why did you bring us up out of Egypt to this terrible place? It has no grain or figs, grape-vines or pomegranates. And there is no water to drink!" (Num. 20:5). Here was another opportunity for Moses to highlight the Lord's capacity to provide.

The instructions Moses receives make sense here in this place. The Lord directs Moses to take his staff in hand and speak to the rock, and when he does, the Lord will bring forth a surge of water from it. These instructions differ from the instructions Moses had received earlier in the southern Sinai (Exod. 17:1–6). There the predominant geological formation was granite, metamorphic rock too tightly compressed to hold water. When Moses struck the rock at Rephidim and water came out, it demonstrated Moses's trust and honored the Lord.

Here in the Wilderness of Zin, Moses lost the privilege of leading Israel into the promised land.

But the geology of the Wilderness of Zin is different. Here meager rainfall flows vertically through the porous limestone until it encounters a flinty seam. The water then travels horizontally until it exits the cliff face. However, when evaporation causes a mineral cap to form at the exit point, the water stops flowing. Water then builds up under increasing pressure until the moment when someone breaks the cap, producing a gush of water from the rock. That's why the Lord instructed Moses to speak to the rock in the Wilderness of Zin rather than strike it.

Read carefully and you will see that Moses did the opposite. He took his staff in hand and struck the rock. He played it safe, trusting his own ability to read the rock more than the Lord's ability to do a miracle. This diverted honor from the Lord onto himself—a grievous failure in leadership that led to Moses's disqualification.

We still see this happening in the church today. Self-aggrandizing church leaders who call attention to themselves show a lack of trust in the Lord and take the honor due him. Harm to the church naturally follows. This is a time to pray for our leaders, asking the Lord to build in them the kind of humility and trust that was missing in Moses.

🐝 How has the geology of this story changed the way you read it?

🐝 How can you encourage your church leaders to remain faithful to their call?

Dear Lord, thank you for the church leaders who get it right. Please bless them in all their efforts to trust you, and encourage us to praise you for all you do for us.

Southern Wilderness

Makhtesh Ramon

DEUTERONOMY 8:1–3

Remember how the LORD your God led you all the way in the
wilderness these forty years, to humble and test you in order
to know what was in your heart . . . to teach you that man does
not live on bread alone but on every word that comes from the
mouth of the LORD.

Deuteronomy 8:2–3

The sprawling moonscape of Makhtesh Ramon
(Ramon Crater) takes its name from a household
utensil. In Hebrew, *makhtesh* is a bowl used with a
pestle for small grinding tasks. This canyon is infinitely larger,
but its near-vertical cliff faces resemble the shape of a *makhtesh*.
It's a wonderful place to get a sense for the southern wilderness
of the Holy Land. The view from the canyon rim captures the
impression that the prophet Jeremiah sought to convey with
words when he called it "the barren wilderness . . . , a land of
deserts and ravines, a land of drought and utter darkness, a
land where no one travels and no one lives" (Jer. 2:6).

The Lord brought Israel through the Wilderness of Paran in order to humble, test, and teach them.

Why did the Lord invest thirty-eight years of Israel's time in such a wilderness? Moses answers that question in the opening verses of Deuteronomy 2. This experience had three dimensions. First, the wilderness humbles Israel. In Egypt, the tallest things on the horizon had celebrated human accomplishment. In the wilderness, mortals quickly reached the limits of their abilities, a humbling experience.

Second, the wilderness tests Israel. Here, where there are no grainfields, no water sources, no people, the Lord asks, "Will you trust me now when the fundamentals for survival are not in view?"

Third, the wilderness teaches Israel. It teaches them that the Lord is both willing and able to provide for their needs in a land that doesn't produce. Bread in hand is good. A promise from God is better.

The wilderness isn't just a geographical region, though. It can also be a season of life. It's those times when circumstances spin beyond our control. It's those times when our physical, mental, and emotional well-being are threatened. That's when we are quick to ask, as did God's people in the past, "Why, Lord? Why have you brought us to this place?"

I've found a better set of questions to ask, ones prompted by the three purposes for which the Lord took Israel into the wilderness: Do we need humbling? Does our faith need testing to reveal how strong it is? Do we need to learn afresh how willing and capable the Lord is to provide for us when we cannot provide for ourselves?

❧ Describe a time in your life when you were in a season of wilderness.

❧ How have you seen the Lord use a wilderness season to shape your character and faith?

Lord, I don't like being in a season of wilderness, but I trust you. Use my wilderness seasons to humble me, to test me, and to teach me. Give me the wisdom to see how you are using wilderness in my life, and may I be the better for it.

Israel

2 KINGS 5:1–19

> "Go in peace," Elisha said.
> 2 Kings 5:19

It has ended more quickly than you imagined it could. The trip of a lifetime is over and it's time to go home. As you sit at the airport gate waiting on your flight or as you prepare to set this book aside, let's reflect on why the Lord has taken you on this trip. Remember, your journey through the Holy Land hasn't been happenstance. The Lord brings people here to show them this land and change them through the experience.

Naaman was one such person. He wasn't a descendant of Abraham or a resident of ancient Israel. He was from Aram, a country northeast of the Holy Land. And like you, he was a visitor who came and then left. But he didn't return home as the same person who left.

There were many things in Naaman's life he wouldn't want changed. The Bible tells us he was a "great man" who was "highly regarded," "a valiant soldier" with repeated victories to his credit (2 Kings 5:1). No need for change there.

Sunset on the Mediterranean Sea marks our return home.

But he traveled to Israel with two problems that had gone unaddressed in his homeland. Naaman was afflicted with a skin disease that no one in Aram could cure. What's more, Naaman's homeland couldn't teach him who God is or how he regards sinners. This man with the debilitating skin disease was burdened by guilt and fear of divine punishment.

The Lord brought Naaman to Israel to change all that. When Naaman arrived, the prophet Elisha directed him to wash seven times in the Jordan River. When Naaman did so, "his flesh was restored and became clean like that of a young boy" (2 Kings 5:14). And because this miraculous healing came from the hand of the Lord, Naaman's impression about the divine was also changing. This Aramean commander declared, "Now I know that there is no God in all the world except in Israel" (5:15).

This changed man left the Holy Land and returned to his homeland and the familiar rhythms of his former life. But he didn't return the same man who had left. The healed Naaman knew God and lived at peace with him.

It will take a few days, but once you unpack your bags or put down this book, things will start returning to normal. Home will feel like home. You will go back to washing your own dishes and taking out the garbage. You will return to working and paying the bills. But I pray things won't become too normal. Like Naaman, the Lord has taken you for this walk in the Holy Land to change you. That means you will never be the person you were before you began this journey.

Go in peace.

🌿 What changes were you expecting because of your time in Israel?

🌿 What new insights or changes surprised you?

Lord, I honor the fact that you bring people to Israel to change them just as you did Naaman. As I return to the normal rhythms of life, help me appreciate and live out the changes at work in me.

IMAGE CREDITS

Maps on pages 15, 26, 58, 74, 103, 127, 213, 224, 280 are by International Mapping and are copyright © Baker Publishing Group.

Photos on pages 18, 88, 266 are copyright © Baker Publishing Group. Collection of the Israel Museum, Jerusalem, and courtesy of the Israel Antiquities Authority. Exhibited at the Israel Museum, Jerusalem.

Photos on pages 22, 30, 39, 50, 70, 78, 100, 115, 135, 143, 147, 154, 161, 165, 173, 176, 183, 190, 194, 198, 202, 206, 209, 221, 228, 235, 242, 245, 248, 255, 259, 263, 269, 287 are copyright © John A. Beck.

Photos and illustrations on pages 34, 42, 46, 55, 62, 67, 81, 84, 92, 107, 111, 119, 123, 132, 139, 150, 158, 169, 180, 186, 239, 251, 273, 276, 284, 291, 294 are copyright © Baker Publishing Group.

Photo on page 95 is copyright © Paul Wright.

Photo on page 217 is copyright © Baker Publishing Group. Courtesy of the British Museum, London, England.

Photo on page 232 is copyright © Baker Publishing Group. Courtesy of Musée du Louvre; Autorisation de photographer et de filmer. Louvre, Paris, France.

John A. Beck (PhD, Trinity International University) has taught courses in Hebrew and Old Testament for more than twenty-five years, many of those years teaching field studies in Israel, Jordan, and Egypt. Beck spends most of his year writing and is a permanent adjunct faculty member at Jerusalem University College in Israel. His books include *The Basic Bible Atlas*, *Along the Road*, *The Baker Illustrated Guide to Everyday Life in Bible Times*, and *The Holy Land for Christian Travelers*. Learn more at JohnABeckAuthor.com.

"A masterful guide to the lands of the Bible."

—PAUL H. WRIGHT,
president, Jerusalem University College, Israel

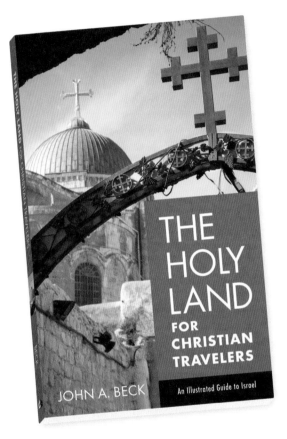

The Holy Land for Christian Travelers puts a biblical scholar
and experienced Holy Land guide at your side to ensure
that you not only find the sites you want to visit but also
understand their biblical significance.

1266 Riala Circle
CAMP VERDE
    AZ 86322
Audrey &
C/O George Elliott

520 - 465 - 5895

Explore the land of the Bible
AS NEVER BEFORE

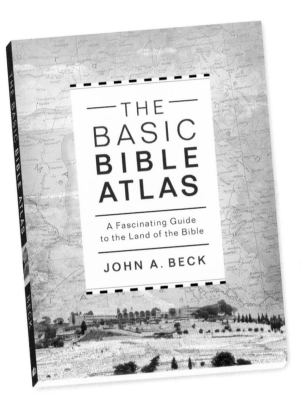

To begin to fully understand the Bible, we must understand the geographical settings of Scripture and how each place participates in the biblical story. With its colorful maps and illustrations, *The Basic Bible Atlas* helps us do just that, so we can appreciate how place impacted events in the Bible.

JOHNABECKAUTHOR.COM

For more information on John A. Beck's books and speaking, and to sign up for his newsletter, visit him online.